The

The Edinburgh Establishment

v

Celtic

Also by the same author:

Books:

The Football Club: Celtic first, last and always (2002-out of print)

Planes, Trains and Martin O'Neill (2003-out of print)

From Albert, With Love (2011)

Dougie, Dougie (2011)

Wim's Tims (2011)

Albert, Dougie and Wim (Compendium of previous three books-2012)

Poles 'N' Goals and Hesselink (2012)

By Any Means Necessary: Journey with Celtic Bampots (2012)

The Last Pearl Diver (2013)

Anyone but Celtic: Inside the culture that created the Lanarkshire Referees Association.

Short Stories that have appeared in print:

Coasters (2008)

When you Yank a Metropolitan (2013)

Soundtrack of the New York Waterfall (2013)

Films

The Asterisk Years (2014)

Future Projects

Anyone but Celtic (Film, 2016)

E********* (Book, 2016)

P***** D****** (Film, 2017)

Website:

www.ls86productions.com

Twitter:

@Paullarkin74

Facebook Group:

'Paul Larkin Books'

Foreword

*An Asterisk. From Late Latin asteriscus, from ancient Greek asteriskos. Like a little star it resembles a conventional image of star. To indicate an omission.

How very apt like five stars on a football jersey.

Why do you try to cheat?
And trample people under your feet
Don't you know it is wrong?
To cheat the trying man
Don't you know it is wrong?
To cheat the trying man
Well you better stop, it is the wrong 'em boyo

You lie, steal, cheat and deceit
In such a small, small game
Don't you know it is wrong
To cheat the trying man
Don't you know it is wrong?
To cheat the trying man
You better stop, it is the wrong 'em boyo

The Clash-Wrong Em Boyo

Average Joe Miller

November 2015

A note from the Author

It all started one afternoon in Lisbon...

There were many, many victims of this corruption. A corruption that, even now, is denied by many.

Tommy Burns hair went white trying to stop a Rangers team that had an enormous advantage over him in that unlimited overdraft the Bank of Scotland were providing not long after trying to shut us down for a fraction of what Rangers owed them. We heard on *Hail Hail Media* how much Tommy meant to McNamara and Donnelly and how their biggest regret in football was not winning a title for Tommy.

It didn't have to be like that.

Kris O'Neil was an aspiring Hearts player in 1998, made his debut at Ibrox after sweeping all before him at youth level. Come 2000 he was starting to establish himself as a first team player when the rug was pulled from under him by Craig Levein and he was released. Everyone was spending big money and there wasn't any room for player development at Tynecastle.

It didn't have to be like that.

Dunfermline fans had no idea that David Murray could pull strings at their club. They had no idea that Jimmy Calderwood was a Murray appointment or that Scott Wilson and Barry Nicholson were handed to them, with contracts already in place, by Murray. Other players on big money came in and would eventually lead to a financial meltdown at the club. A club owned by a man who was allegedly a financial expert.

It didn't have to be like that.

Hibs came back up in 1999 and before long were buying players like David Zitelli. Such was the spending going on everywhere else they knew they had to step up. This would lead to club finances spiralling out of control and having no choice but to sell and bring through youth players. These players get experience and talent like Riordan, O'Connor, Thomson and Brown. This makes Hibs a good team. Except finance dictates that they have to sell all these players and eventually end up back in the Championship.

It didn't have to be like that.

Right now Scottish football is at a precipice. Our own club still runs at a Champions League level in terms of wages but for how much longer? Scottish football is in a dreadful mess. All of it is a consequence of the mirage that David Murray created when the media were happy to not scrutinise and instead paint a picture of a modern day King Midas. The main point of *The Asterisk Years* was to change the narrative regarding Murray and leave people with no doubt he caused it all. Everything Murray did was built on sand and as soon as the global financial crisis happened people soon realised that this was not an empire upon which the sun would never set, this was a house of cards with *The Sun* and *Daily Record* as its pets.

What matters now is justice. We know we will never get the trophies back we should have won and nor will any of the others that faced Rangers teams they should never have. However, it will forever remain a stain on Scottish football as long as Rangers (IL) are not stripped of every trophy they won in that era. Celtic should be at the forefront of that fight otherwise, what's the point?

Right now, David Murray has got away with most of this, sure his companies were broken up and hived off, he no longer resides in Murrayfield and his Charlotte Square vanity office is long gone but this man singlehandedly broke Scottish football, destroyed the Bank of Scotland and the lives of many people and is yet to face any sort of justice.

It doesn't have to be like that

The day we expected to finally get justice, after suffering a decade of cheating, we saw Rangers (IL) fans punch the air in triumph despite a guilty verdict. The "punishment" from Lord Nimmo-Smith and his panel was so laughable, it would be funny if it wasn't so serious. One thing I've learnt now more than ever is we cannot expect help from anywhere. We have to do things ourselves. So, that's what I have done. What started as a look into the Lord Nimmo-Smith case has ended up as a look at the whole Murray era and what I found both staggered me and angered me. First of all, and most galling for me, was that I realised the Axis of Evil that raged against us in the era of 1988-2011 all came from around two miles from my own house. That's also where Lord Nimmo-Smith stays as well by the way. You'll find out more about that later. This all enrages me because I now feel I could have done something, anything, to try and stop it. Of course, as you read on, you'll know that I couldn't simply due to the power of these men and the fact that I was a young idiot through most of this era who couldn't do jack shit.

Then something strange happened to me. I was contacted by someone ... let us call him 'Bob'. There has been so much speculation about this guy but I will never reveal who he is. This person was part of something I was a little aware of existing but knew next to fuck all about. At first I thought it was a crank as I have been known to be contacted by a few in my time but of hours of conversation, some rules set down and some discreet research by myself, I realised this person was legit. As he told me the stories, facts and figures that you are about to read in this book, I knew I had to get them out there. It has taken us a year, a lot of worry, some frantic phone calls, flights to mysterious locations and brass balls, but we have done it. The person, for obvious reasons, remains in anonymity.

What you are about to read is the revised story of how David Murray put a stranglehold not just on Scottish football but Scottish society in an attempt to put Rangers to the top of European football.

And how we beat them...

Paul Larkin
December 2015

For all the victims.

All truth passes through three stages. First it is ridiculed. Second, it is violently opposed. Third, it is accepted as being self-evident.

Arthur Schopenhauer

1-Ridicule

As soon as your born they make you feel small,

By giving you no time instead of it all,

Till the pain is so big you feel nothing at all,

A working class hero is something to be,

They hurt you at home and they hit you at school,

They hate you if you're clever and they despise a fool,

Till you're so fucking crazy you can't follow their rules,

A working class hero is something to be,

When Andy Walker ruled the world

Most supporters will have an era where they will say "That was my time that was my team". For me, that will always be season 1987/88. I often use the wonderful *Celtic Wiki* to trigger memories and brush up on facts but not this time, this season will forever be imprinted on my mind.

Of course, I did not know at the time just what lay ahead and that dark arts were already in play by end of that season designed to ensure Celtic never won a *trophy* again never mind a double. Whilst we were celebrating at Hampden in the Sun, David Murray had already began talks with Lawrence Marlborough that would lead to the purchase of Rangers on November 23rd 1988 for a fee of £6m. A fee that Murray borrowed to make the deal happen but you didn't read that at that at the time of course.

It all started the year before when something weird happened in Scottish football, Rangers won the league. This was practically unheard of when I was growing up. The last time they had won it was 1978 and I didn't remember that so this was all new to me. The thing is, they should never have won it in 87. We had a six point lead in February, when it was two points for a win, and wanted to sign Joe McLaughlin and Pat Nevin from Chelsea for the final push. Except the board decided that if manager Davie Hay wanted them, he would need to pay for them out of his of own pocket. To be fair, it almost worked for Billy Beane. We stuttered after that and, despite destroying Rangers at Celtic Park, when they were convinced they would win there for only the second time in the 80s (An insight into our dominance over them in the 80s comes from the fact that in the entire decade, Rangers only won twice at Celtic Park and both wins come courtesy of flukey strikes, one from Alex Miller and one from Ian Ferguson) and that day, when we lost at home to Falkirk and Rangers got a point at Pittodrie, it was treated like a family death in our house.

Something had to be done.

Incredibly, it was.

A few weeks later it emerged that Cesar himself was on his way back. A deal had been struck by Billy McNeill and then chairman, Jack McGinn, in a Fine Fare supermarket car park in Clydebank. When the news broke, I think that was the only time I saw my father cry. If anyone could sort things, it was big Billy.

It has to be said, the initial signings didn't inspire anyone. The first signing was Billy Stark. Mick McCarthy had actually been signed by Davie Hay, who was eased out the door by the board sharpish, but Mick had worked with Billy before so there wasn't a problem. Billy McNeill deliberately didn't publicise the signing of Stark right, now 30, as he wanted a proper message sent out to the fans. So all new signings were unveiled at the same time, Mick McCarthy, Billy Stark, goal machine from Motherwell Andy Walker and Chris Morris from Sheffield Wednesday.

When the picture of all four appeared in the paper the next day, my auld man looked at it and said "Who the fuck is Chris Morris?"

We had a decent start. A 4-0 opening day win at Cappielow was followed up with a 1-0 win over Hearts, a 1-0 win that saw Hearts owner, Wallace Mercer, go berserk over the lack of a linesman's flag for our winner (Mark McGhee had shoulder barged Dave McPherson) and the lack of a penalty when Robertson went down a little too easily in the box.

The big test would come on Aug 29th, when more expensive Souness signings came to Celtic Park, but one of the most exciting things of my life happened the week before, in fact, two.

We had gone to East End Park on Aug 22 to play newly promoted Dunfermline. Our bus has the most people on a single decker I have ever seen. There were around 5000 Celtic supporters locked out that day but I had a ticket. Not only that, my ticket came from a Celtic player, an actual first team player who would be playing that day. I almost fainted with the excitement. It had nothing to do with me by the way. It came from another of Archie Wright's grandson's, Stephen, who got two for the centre stand from Mark McGhee. First of all, I'd never been in the centre stand of any ground in my life. Secondly, despite me being 13 and Stephen being 15, we were allowed to go in ourselves. All this would have been enough to keep my school mates going for weeks but on the way in we also spoke to Archie MacPherson.

In those days, as I've written before, you weren't saturated with live football on TV. In fact, you weren't even saturated with football highlights in Scotland. No change there then.

At this time of the season, Sportscene hadn't even started for the season so when we saw Archie, we asked him, "When does Sportscene start Archie?" to which he replied, without breaking stride, "Next Saturday son"

That next Saturday was when Rangers were due in Paradise and that was, funnily enough, the first game Sportscene showed. I've said this before but that 1-0 win was probably the biggest gubbing I ever saw us give them. We absolutely destroyed them that day with Paul McStay in majestic form. The only goal came in four minutes, a Mark McGhee cross was dummied by Peter Grant and Billy Stark hit a beauty right into Chris Woods' right hand corner.

Even better was to follow.

It has hard to over egg just how much Celtic supporters despised Graeme Souness then. He was the antipathy of everything we stood for. He was an arrogant, strutting, Tory wanker. He was an animal on the park. I only saw him get the better of Paul McStay once, in a game at Ibrox in January 1987, and I don't think Paul ever forgave him. He used to run Souness ragged in midfield at will but my favourite McStay/Souness moment came the season after in the 1989 Scottish Cup Final. 1-0 down to us, Souness subbed himself on in an "I'll handle this" type way. He strutted onto the pitch, got to the centre circle and demanded the ball. It came to him and he was already looking up, seeing where he would pass it to and grab the equaliser he was born to create. At the point where he was about to collect the ball, Paul McStay came in with a tackle that was akin to watching a speeding train go past you whilst you're on the platform. Cleanly taking the ball, he left Souness in a crumpled heap and the moustached one didn't touch the ball for the rest of the game.

I've said it before and I'll say it again, don't let anyone kid you otherwise, Paul McStay was a fucking genius.

So in this game in August 87, we were playing keep ball in the middle of the park. Billy Stark had even lost a boot and was still participating when Souness, looking like he'd never played the game before, lost it and tried to maim Billy Stark's bootless foot. Now, what I love about this incident more than anything, is the fact that when Souness did this, Chris Morris and Roy Aitken immediately attacked Souness. That's how it should be, it's a band of brothers and you should be ready to die beside the guy next to you. Especially if the enemy has just attacked. Things calmed down, slightly, when Davie Syme flashed a red card at Souness. As he walks off the pitch, the TV cameras capture the Celtic end in deep, deep joy as the arch enemy is slain.

Football was made for moments like that.

Our form after that was scratchy. We went out The Skol Cup at Pittodrie the following Wednesday, then drew 0-0 at Tannadice before a weird game at Brockville saw the great Tommy Burns score with his right foot to grab us a 1-0 win that really should have been 10 in the first half alone.

We brought in Frank McAvennie at a time when the fans were desperate for the club to bring back Charlie Nicholas. You have to remember that, due to a TV strike in England, not many were aware of just how good Frank was.

Things sort of stumbled on a bit from then. We went out the UEFA Cup to Borussia Dortmund and the season seemed in grave danger of going completely off the rails. What always gets lost from the infamous 2-2 game at Ibrox (apart from the fact that Rangers should have had their entire team sent off and Peter Grant should have scored a hat-trick), when McAvennie, Woods and Butcher were sent off, is that we blew a two goal lead against nine men. Ok, we only had ten but still. We dominated most of the game and still only got a point.

We followed up that game with a 2-1 home defeat to Dundee Utd and 3-2 home win over Falkirk that saw fans in the main stand chanting "Charlie, Charlie" at Billy McNeill and fans on our bus speculate that the club was sliding back to "1978 terms" when Rangers had won the treble and we had finished 5th.

In any success, victory or won battle, there is always a turning point and ours came on Halloween.

Going up to Pittodrie on that day, no one felt that confident. A lot of folk think

Aberdeen collapsed the second Alex Ferguson walked out the door. The reality is, they were a very good team for a good eight years after that so going up there was always tough. It was a very tight game, with defences well on top and looked to be heading for a 0-0 draw when a rare Willie Miller/Robert Connor mistake saw McAvennie nip in with eighteen minutes to go and grab us the points. I can still feel the elation and excitement as we travelled home that night, and from then on, we didn't look back.

The final piece of the jigsaw that season was also soon to arrive.

In the week after grabbed a brave point at Tynecastle, Mark McGhee equalising after Mick McCarthy had been sent off, and we all streamed along Gorgie Road after the game singing "Who do you think you are kidding, Wallace Mercer? If you think we are on the run" after Mercer had claimed that week that Hearts had Celtic "on the run".

Football will fucking stop before that ever happens.

Celtic always had a great habit of signing folk on a Friday before a home game so to boost the crowd so when news broke on a Friday that we had paid £650,000 for the hottest young talent in Scottish football, Joe Miller, there was a genuine sense of anticipation. It was also made all the more pleasing as Alex Ferguson went berserk when he found out. He claimed that he had a deal with Aberdeen that he would not touch any of their players when he left for Manchester United, on the proviso that he got first dibs on Joe Miller if Aberdeen ever wanted to sell. In his usual restrained form, he said it was now "open season" on all Aberdeen players and not long after the Miller deal, he signed Jim Leighton. The hits just kept on coming.

Joe's debut came the following day against Dundee and kept up his remarkable record of scoring every time he played at Celtic Park. That record would only last another week but still. The Dundee game was one of those game you never forget. Big, noisy crowd, two up in the first five minutes and the debutant gets a goal. All three strikers scored that day, primarily because they were all on fire.

It's funny to think now about just how much love I had for Andy Walker then. I even bought one of those pen pictures of him and had it on my wall for years, way after he left as well. You see my first football hero, Danny McGrain, had left in the summer and I was on the hunt for a new one. When Andy Walker signed for us, it had in the paper that he had gone to school with Billy McNeill's daughter. "That'll do for me" was my Uncle Francey's reaction. He came into the club and, from the minute he set foot on the pitch, he started scoring goals. All sorts of goals. He could head it and was a brilliant penalty box striker who could also take a ball on a run and go past the last defender before dispatching the ball past a goalie with little fuss. The perfect example of that was in *that* 2-2 draw at Ibrox where he outpaced Terry Butcher with a fantastic touch before calmly slotting the ball in the bottom corner. It was past Graham Roberts but Jock Brown, commentating, said "That would have beaten even a top class goalkeeper"

His biggest talent though was reading the game. He had an uncanny knack of being in the right place at the right time, Klondyke for a striker, and would always gamble on a mistake from a defender or goalie. 87/88 was his year in the sun because the following season he got a bad eye injury towards the end of the season at Pittodrie and I never felt he was the same again. Seeing him come back again in 1994 was like seeing the girl you loved who left you come back drunk to try and win you back by dirty dancing you in the pub and then collapsing in a heap.

As we moved into the actual year of 1988, indications that this was going to be a year we would never forget were actually few and far between. We followed up the glorious New Year 2-0 win against Rangers with an insipid 1-1 draw at Love Street and our goal actually came from Campbell Money making a complete arse of a cross and dropping it in his own net. Uninspiring home wins against Stranraer in the cup plus Motherwell and Morton in the league, all 1-0 wins that the opposition can feel aggrieved about given how well they had played except for Motherwell who broke the world record for passes back to the keeper, saw the fans get restless as Rangers kept that cheque book at the ready with big signings like Richard Gough and Mark Walters (shamefully treated by some "fans" on his debut at Celtic Park who replicated the treatment that Everton fans had given John Barnes earlier that season by throwing bananas at him) who, it has to be said, were both tremendous players. Although the asterisk years were not yet upon us, they were in the post.

Except this is Celtic.

I've often written the above and then gone on to write some tale of woe, so it gives me genuine delight to talk about that other aspect of Celtic that has laced through the club's history like Donald Duck for Walt Disney, sometimes just sometimes, everything goes right.

Just as we scraped a few wins at Easter Road in the cup and Dens Park in the league, just as fans started to get the odd squeaky bum now and again, everything clicked into place.

The month of March was glorious, we played well and trounced teams like Dunfermline, Falkirk and Partick (cup) and rolled up at Ibrox for a live TV match (unheard of in those days) knowing a win would almost certainly see the title coming back to Paradise. We went into the game four points clear (in the days of two points for a win) with a game in hand, which was at Pittodrie so carried no guarantees whatsoever, but in fine form. Rangers though were at home and simply had to win. We also had not won at Ibrox since January 1st 1985 so no one was taking anything for granted.

Pre-match there was an incredible story of a Catholic Priest, who also happened to be a Rangers season ticket holder, remember this was March 1988, that probably baffled most of Scotland, whatever side of the pole you happened to fall on.

I was in the main stand at Ibrox that day, no not another kamikaze mission, back then Celtic got all the Broomloan, half the main stand and one of the enclosures (in the really dark days for Rangers we also got a fair bit of the Govan stand too) and was as pissed off as everyone else who didn't get a ticket for the Broomloan was.

It has to be said that Rangers played very well in the first half with the two Dick's, I mean Ian's, Durrant and Ferguson combining well a few times. We were making sloppy errors and looked a wee bit nervous if truth be told. This was also the first game we had played at Ibrox since that 2-2 draw and it did look like players were doing their very best to keep a lid on it.

Just before the end of the first half there was a little sign of things to come. Paul McStay let rip with a 30 yarder that Chris Woods just managed to tip over the bar. Suddenly, with The Maestro pulling the strings, we were in complete control of the game within five minutes of the re-start.

Sitting in the stand, like most others, I was a nervous wreck. This meant more than any game since Love Street 86 (you may have heard me mention that now and again) and it looked like we were on the up with less than 25 minutes to go. With 23 minutes to go, that was rubber stamped by, who else, Paul McStay who scored with a volley that was only bettered by his celebration. The sheer ecstasy on Paul's face as he ran towards the Celtic support in the Broomloan (see?) was a joy to behold. Us lot in the main stand were going just as berserk just you felt that little bit detached from it all.

We would get our own back.

Before that though, six minutes later, Jan Bartram equalised with a speculative shot that went through a crowd of bodies and squeezed past Packie Bonner. The Dane would later take on legendary status with Celtic support though after being thrown out of Ibrox for calling Graeme Souness a "Dirty Bastard" which is like being thrown out of the Coliseum for saying it is too violent.

A draw would have done us if truth be told. However the equalizer seemed to just de-rail us for a small time as within five minutes, we were back in front. A Tommy Burns corner was met by the head of Anton Rogan who managed to bullet a header, eh, right onto the chest of Andy Walker and it bounced from there right into the net.

Oh how we laughed.

The next 12 minutes were spent in sheer agony, Rangers didn't really threaten us but we knew the magnitude of this potential win. One of the Bhoys from our bus, Jason Allan, actually got up and left as he simply couldn't bear it. Even when I saw him on the bus afterwards he was still in bits and I couldn't blame him, it was that sort of day. I don't remember how I felt at the full time whistle that day but it was probably relief. I'd first gone to Ibrox in May 1983, we won that day of course, but I'd only seen two wins since there since, both 2-1 victories, so I needed another. I do remember how I felt as I walked down the old wooden steps coming out of Ibrox that day. I cried. I cried a lot that season because lots of people cried at football matches in those days, mostly tears of joy thankfully, but I when I think back now it does feel like it meant more then. Not because fans now don't care but back then it was far easier for it to encompass your whole life and there were no blogs or facebook pages to express how you felt then, you kept it in until you couldn't anymore.

Plus Celtic was always about fighting against the world.

It was drummed into me as a kid that when Celtic won something, we weren't just beating the team in front of us, we were beating the refs, the media, the rest of Scotland and, of course, the establishment.

Suddenly the dream of a centenary year championship was becoming a reality. More weight was added to that belief with a second league win of the season at Pittodrie the following midweek, after a 0-0 draw with Dundee Utd that was never a bad result in those days, again with an Andy Walker winner from an Anton Rogan knock down although this time Andy knew everything about it.

And so did We.

That night in the Beach End at Pittodrie was the first time the song "Championees oh we are we are we" was sung with real gusto and from then on trying to stop our title challenge was like trying to hold back the tide. There was also the small matter of a cup semi-final against Hearts to come and the real possibility of a centenary double. If you want to point at something as evidence as of how Scottish football has changed in the last 25 years, then this Hearts semi is as good an example as any. It was played on a Saturday afternoon at 3pm, cost £3 to get in and attracted a crowd of exactly 65,000 people. That said, I was also at the final that year which had an official crowd of 74,000 and the idea that you could have fitted another 9000 people into Hampden for the Hearts game was akin to filling a phone box tight with folk then suggesting you could find room for another nine.

The Hearts game was as incredible a game as you'll see anywhere. Paul McStay had arguably his finest game in the hoops whilst Frank McAvennie had undoubtedly his worst. Time and again The Maestro would weave his way through the Hearts defence and lay passes on for Macca like a silver service waiter lays cutlery and Macca would blaze it wide or over the bar or tamely to Hearts goalie Henry Smith. The inevitable happened and Hearts scored. A speculative Brian Whittaker cross flew past Pat Bonner, who was being assaulted by Dave McPherson at the time, and Hearts were one up with an hour on the clock. People think that Celtic fans have always had a strong hatred for Hearts but the simply isn't true. Primarily the reason is from the early 60's up until 1986, Hearts were never a threat to us. We never played them in any cup finals, at the time of writing since 1956, and they never appeared on the radar until 1986 which, for a Tim from Edinburgh, suited me fine. That being said, the team we were playing that day had a strong Rangers element to it and in their 13 that day, there were no less than four ex Rangers players adding to their management team of Rangers rejects. They also sang, with incredible gusto, at Hampden that day the song "Oh Edinburgh is wonderful, apart from Hibs, Coons and Pakis, Edinburgh is wonderful". So, to be one down to this shower of bastards, added to how much a misery my life would be, it's fair to say fear had gripped me by now.

One other thing should be said just now. Hampden was often a chance for my mates to come and see Celtic or at least go to the game. It was affordable and it was an occasion. I had Tims and non-Tims with me at Hampden in the late 80's and early 90's and it did feel like a proper event. Once, when I was in the Aberdeen end at a Celtic game at Pittodrie, I became aware of the fact that this entitled me to a ticket for a Celtic v Aberdeen league cup semi-final for the Aberdeen end at Hampden in an era when they would sell out. I spoke to a mate of mine at school, Dennis, and asked him if he wanted to go? He was an Aberdeen fan but came from a family that were struggling a lot and never really had the opportunity to get to their games. He said yes and the following day he produced the fiver required for the ticket. I gave it to my Ma who sent a cheque up to Pittodrie and the ticket appeared about five days later. (I have wondered on occasion what Aberdeen thought of me. Here I was buying tickets for the Aberdeen end for two games v Celtic in quick succession, Aberdeen won one and drew one and I never ever bought an official ticket from them again, probably sitting in the ticket office thinking "Hard to please this cunt") Dennis came through on my supporters bus, £1 for 16 and under, and went round to the Aberdeen end. They won the game but the point is, it was affordable to go and it was easily accessible then as well. Similar scenario in 1992 when my mate Hosey came with me to a Celtic v Rangers semi-final at Hampden. I've documented both these stories in other books but from different angles. I just can't imagine nowadays saying to a fan of another team "Come along to Hampden with me, it's £13 for the train and £30 for the ticket" there's not a chance fans of other teams would be interested in that "here for the beer" mentality Hosey had that night simply because that beer, when you take in the whole day's spend, is going to cost his entire disposable income for a week.

A mate who was a Tim though was Goges. We stood pensively on that terracing at Hampden, section N, and willing Celtic to score. It looked forlorn it has to be said. With two minutes to go and nerves frayed like the bottom of a pair of jeans that are an inch too long, we got a corner. Tommy Burns raced over to take it and Roy Aitken shouted "Tommy, get it in here" pointing just in front of where he was standing at the front post. Tommy duly obliged but the ball broke and players from both teams frantically tried to get at the ball with Roy somehow managing to eek it past a few Hearts players and lay it off to Mark McGhee. If we thought that was good, what Mark then did with the ball was Olympian. Despite seven Hearts players standing in front of him, Mark somehow managed to guide a shot through them all like a fucking drone missile, before those were fashionable as well, right into the net. To say we went into total delirium is like saying Howard Marks likes Ganja. At the point the ball hit the net, I jumped up and promptly fell down. As I looked up I saw lots of bodies jumping up and down as I did anything I could to get myself back up although did feel like some daft cunt who had fallen in Pamplona. Thankfully Goges had spotted me and being a big bloke even then he was able to pick me up to the light again after the darkness of cunts trampling all over me and I got my eye level on the pitch just as Frank McAvennie was crossing in ball that Henry Smith caught, was challenged by Mark McGhee, dropped and then Andy Walker blasted into the net and the game was ours. Goges promptly dropped me.

People may laugh or pour scorn on my hero worship for Andy Walker then but for those keeping score, that's three late winners in three weeks against Rangers, Aberdeen and Hearts. What's not to love?

As you all know, the rest of the season was spent in total bliss. The league was clinched against Dundee and the double against Dundee Utd. Andy Walker scored two in 60 seconds against Dundee to send Paradise into raptures and Frank McAvennie made up for that semi-final horror show by hitting a brace at Hampden in the sun and capturing that centenary double.

Andy Walker showed fleeting glimpses of that season in the future but never was the same player again.

Me, I was blissfully happy. I didn't know the meteor that was coming to hit me, Celtic, Celtic supporters and pretty much most of Scottish football was almost upon us.

Old School

Primary school I loved. High school I hated. In Primary school I had great friends, I did well with my work and I kissed quite a few of the girls there. High school was pretty much a write off for me and most of the folk in my class as well. When I think about it, the thing that I didn't get then was that school was about arming you with the tools to go out in the world to create as many opportunities for yourself as possible. I should put emphasis on the word *create* because that's what you have to do when you are fighting from day one. None of us had the first clue what hurdles we would have to jump on life nor that they would be a lot higher than they would be for us than they would be for those who went to better schools.

I know some (Ok, probably the three folk who would never admit to buying anything I do) may read this book and think "Who does the cunt think he is, *Oliver*?" but the thing about what you read in my books, whether it makes me look like a pimp, player or prick, it's all real. So don't blame me for your middle class guilt you cunts.

Secondary school days for me started with the breakfast club. For 10p you got a hamburger, sausage, black pudding or bacon roll and for 5p you could get a cup of tea or milk (no one and I mean no one in my bit had even heard of coffee then never mind paid £3.99 for a cup of the fucking thing) and this was all based in the canteen of the school, Craigroyston Community High School, the first community high school in Britain which meant there was no religion of any kind taught and the thinking behind the school was to encompass everyone from the community.

What a crock of shit that was.

Most of the teachers were sadists who routinely beat the pupils up, swore at them and openly told them they would achieve nothing. Don't get me wrong, a lot of us, me included, were no angels but when you are 12 years old nor should you be. I was beaten up twice by teachers in my time there. Once by a complete lunatic who seemed to spend half his life at his Spanish villa(a cunt who couldn't teach primary 1 kids the way to the sand pit, a fucking Spanish villa) and the other half sending us to the shops to get his lunch for him. One day he took me outside his class and threw me downstairs before kicking the shit out of me. The other teacher who leathered me was a nutcase P.E. Teacher who, completely out of the blue one day, asked in a school corridor if I was threatening him? Before I could decipher what the fuck this cunt was on about, he punched me in the face and kicked me three times as I lay on the ground.

I was 14.

Nothing ever happened about this or any of the other much more savage beatings I saw several pupils get.

At lunch time I always went to my Nana's. She lived just across the road from the school and fed me a staple diet of Granny's Tomato Soup and Ambrosia Creamed Rice. This was a Godsend for my ma and dad's finances let me tell you.

I mentioned the two beatings as they were the most severe but there were plenty of kicks and punches throughout my time there. At the time you just think that's how it is. A lot of pupils were coming from situations that had lots of extreme violence and abuse and school was probably a walk in the park for them compared to home.

Poverty was extreme then too, you realise that now when you look back. I remember any time someone suddenly had money then in the same way, I imagine, I would if someone close to me suddenly won the lottery now. My mates were pretty generous if truth be told. Well, Hosey was at least. In those days if someone had money it would be a trip up to Wimpy and a look round the sports shops then HMV and Virgin. These were very rare occasions though and normally only happened around a birthday time. My two best mates at school, Hosey and Sparky (now known as TCS-That Cunt Sparky) and I all had birthdays close to each other so May and June were golden months. On the nickname for Sparky (which in itself is a nickname) came around about 12-13 years ago when, after years of spending every night in his room with his computer (something I never had until August 2000), he got a bird and ended up marrying her. This meant that the minute he started going out with her, he stopped going out with us (and has kept it going until this day!). Whereas Hosey doesn't need a nickname, one mention of the cunt's name normally has folk rolling their eyes.

Most of my school life was spent going in between their houses and handing in behaviour sheets for school. The only trips were to shitty camps on the west coast of Scotland when, sick of the ritual beatings they gave us, the teachers decided to send us out into the wild in the hope some rabid animal savaged us to death.

I have no good memories from school camp, it was shit and I hated it.

By the end of school, I couldn't wait to get out, which was handy as they couldn't wait to get rid of me. I even had the cheek to stay on for 5th year (what else was I going to do?) after failing all my exams and fannying about for the last four years. I lasted about three weeks when one of the deputy head's who was taking a class one day just said to me on the quiet "Here's some advice, you're not brainy, have no prospects and would be as well leaving now"

So I did.

It was only years later that I found out how most teachers at the school were regarded by community workers and people who knew the school. Lower than a snake's belly. It angered me because although I could misbehave with the best of them, our teachers, in the main, couldn't have cared less the fucking cunts. I take a little of the blame for that but in my defence what I will say is I was a stupid kid who didn't know Jack shit about anything other than playing fitba, watching fitba and loving Celtic. They were getting paid to put us on the straight and narrow educationally.

About five years ago, they bulldozed Craigroyston and built a brand new school on the site, good riddance I say.

I found out in the last few weeks from TCS that the headmaster when we were there, Hugh Mackenzie aka John Wayne (because of the way he walked), wrote a book about being the headmaster at Craigroyston and his sweat and toil in the face of adversity, Thatcherism and the day to day struggle he had as he fought to educate us deranged kids.

As I've slagged TCS in this chapter, I'll leave him with last words on Saint Hugh: "I was at Craigie for six years and I never met the cunt once"

The point of this is not to be autobiographical for the sake of it, it is to paint a picture of school life for someone like me and, no doubt, many millions of others in Scotland. The worst aspect of it is you have no idea how ill-prepared this is making you for life after school. Sport is a good example of that. The only one we really played was football. We dabbled in things like Hockey and even Baseball but football was our thing. I played for the school team throughout and pre-match tactics never got further than "Don't argue with the ref or your opponents, shake hands with everyone after the game" There was no fitness training to speak of, no explanation of the game. In fact I played left midfield mostly because I kicked with the left foot, literally. We all thought we were brilliant right up until we came up against schools from the affluent areas of Edinburgh. They were bigger, stronger, better fed and more aware of football. We had a couple of tremendous players but we were up against it unless playing against schools from Greater Pilton, or areas like Wester Hailes and Niddry. One time we played George Heriots, a fee paying school in Edinburgh and our attitude was "Posh cunts, this will be easy" and then we saw them come off their team bus (They had a team bus FFS!) When I first seen them step off the bus I initially thought they had a big coaching staff (in comparison, our "coach" was also our Maths teacher and he was the guy who didn't want to upset anyone) but I soon realised this was their team. Even I was a skinny wee laddie once as most of our team were and here were these men walking off to take us on. They beat us 9-0, we had four men sent off (including myself) and we had no idea we had just been given a serious lesson in life.

The Custodians

In terms of Celtic, I speak about the centenary year in glowing terms for a lot of reasons and one of them is that it masked a lot of problems at the club at the time (There was a famous cartoon that *Not The View* had over Billy McNeill wallpapering over a cracked wall). Jack McGinn was Chairman but the Kelly, White and Grant control of the club was as strong as it had ever been. The "Biscuit Tin" mentality was alive and well. The club had gone on like this forever and when success came it would mask a pretty amateur set up. Kevin Kelly would boast that the Celtic Pools was worth a million pounds a year to the club but when Rangers started spending that amount on one player then the claim would seem a bit hollow.

There's no doubt that these people made Celtic an easy target. They had lived off Lisbon for years, whilst virtually ignoring the actual Lisbon squad, and seemed to think that everything should be judged on what it was like in 1967. This meant the stadium was dilapidated, training was still going on behind the Celtic Supporters Association and there was even an actual biscuit tin (*Rover* Biscuits) that was passed around the directors after the game to satisfy their sweet teeth whilst the players waited their turn.

Rangers already had a stadium and this gave them a huge advantage as the years unfolded and the tragedy of Hillsborough would see all clubs compelled to have all seater stadia. Our board's answer? To put seats in The Jungle, a move akin to taking the teeth out of a lion.

Lying down after Seville

Even though we are now well past the 10th anniversary of the Seville, there are still some people who have never watched the game back. I am one of them. Similarly, the 4-0 defeat of Kilmarnock at Rugby Park the following Sunday is another game I've not seen since. I was so angry after that game, not sick, sad or let down, angry because, as Chris Sutton said at the time "We knew they'd lie down and they have done". Then, years later, we find out the following: Rangers were paying their players through a tax avoidance scheme. Jimmy Calderwood, Jimmy Nicholl and Sandy Clark, the Dunfermline management team that day they were to lose at Ibrox 6-1, were on a plane to Majorca twenty minutes after the final whistle at Ibrox that day. We know this because Jimmy Calderwood admitted live on Radio Scotland that this was the case. His excuse was "I knew what the conspiracy theorists would make of photos of me congratulating big Alex (McLeish), so me and Jimmy were on a plane twenty minutes later"

Hmm...

First question that springs to my mind is "How did they know?" How did they know they would lose so significantly that day at Ibrox that they would need to be on a plane to Majorca right after the game?

Lots of wee things stand out from that day. Like league goals. You will, of course, be aware of the fact that we lost the league that season by one goal. Henrik Larsson scored 28 league goals in 2002/03. John Hartson scored 18 league goals. Sandwiched between them on 19? Why Stevie Crawford of, you've guessed it, Dunfermline. If anyone has footage of Stevie touching the ball that day at Ibrox, I'd love to see it. On a similar note, there is Derek Stillie of Ayrshire. Not that I am saying Derek's performance was bad that day, but Frank Haffey pissed himself at it. His pathetic attempts at keeping the ball out are summed up at his attempt for the 5th goal when McCann crosses the ball and before it has even got near Stillie, he has fallen down.

We'll come back to that.

Of course, season 2002/03 was no ordinary season and I'm not just talking about Seville. Rangers got more penalties and had more opponents sent off than any other team in any other season in Scottish football history.

If ever a season summed up that something was going on, this was it.

2-Opposed

When they've tortured and scared you for twenty odd years,
Then they expect you to pick a career,
When you can't really function you're so full of fear,
A working class hero is something to be,

Keep you doped with religion and sex and TV,
And you think you're so clever and you're classless and free,
But you're still fucking peasants as far as I can see,
A working class hero is something to be,
A working class hero is something to be.

David Murray and the Edinburgh Establishment

On Wednesday 23rd November 1988, David Murray, a 37 year-old business man from Ayr, bought Rangers Football Club for 6 million pounds.

This purchase was to change forever the football landscape of Scotland and was to make the Establishment Club more a part of the Establishment than any of us could ever have expected ... and more than any of *them* could ever have wanted.

Murray, the man with the Midas touch who received a Knighthood for his unparalleled business acumen, was to be the Ace of Spades in a game of poker that led to the death of Rangers Football Club.

What isn't widely known about Murray is that his first love was rugby. He was a useful player and it was whilst returning from playing in a rugby match that he was involved in the car crash that subsequently led to the loss of his legs.

It is no surprise to those who know the Murray family that, after taking a back seat at Rangers, his Edinburgh-based company, Murray International Holdings, became the main sponsor of the Scottish Rugby Union and, in turn, the Scottish national rugby team.

David Murray is not an Edinburgh man but he has become entirely entangled in the Edinburgh way of operating. Most non-Edinburgh folk, and many of those who are from Edinburgh, never get to see the quiet way it operates through its network of like-minded individuals.

This network is established very early in life as it is incubated in the Edinburgh private school system that encourages a climate of segregation from 'normal' children in the state sector. Having been educated in one of Edinburgh's most expensive private schools for the full 13 years, I know only too well how this network is maintained and enforced.

To give an indication of the importance of these schools to Edinburgh 'culture', it has 16 private schools while greater Glasgow, although boasting more than double the population of Edinburgh, only has 9. In fact, while 7% of children across the UK are privately educated, in Edinburgh that figure is almost 25%.

In Edinburgh, at dinner parties, the most common opening question to another person is not *"what do you do for a living?"* but *"which school did you go to?"* This subtle approach to judging others is what sustains the Edinburgh Old School Tie network. Because, the assumption is, if you went to a private school like I did, then you are 'one of us'.

Even within the private school system there is snobbery. It is loosely based on the cost of school fees but is also linked to the history of the school. It is along those lines that particular school rivalries are formed and acted out on the rugby or cricket field.

Whilst there is a strong sense of rivalry between the private schools, there is a stronger sense of unity through exclusivity. The fact that few state schools focus on rugby and cricket means that the private schools all over Scotland play against each other at these sports.

But the real key to maintaining the 'them and us' feeling is through the very well planned and organised social events.

Central to these events, during the teenage years, are various Balls and Cocktail Parties. At these events, the boys wear full kilt outfits or tuxedos and the girls wear ball gowns. The events are normally held in impressive surroundings such as Hopetoun House, on the outskirts of Edinburgh, and would always be preceded by a cocktail party at the home of one of those attending. It would be normal for around a dozen or so to be invited to the cocktail party and transport would be arranged to get to the venue.

Hopetoun House

These days, many of the private schools are mixed but in David Murray Jnr's day, and certainly in his father's day, many of the schools were boys-only or girls-only. This meant that social events, such as Balls, were one of the best chances for boys to 'interact' with girls!

However, the ultimate aim of these types of events was to act as training for the real dinner parties and cocktail parties that would be held in adult life. This is evidenced by the behaviour of the teenagers at these events. Everyone dressed in 'black tie', drinking some sort of non-alcoholic champagne from a flute (the alcoholic stuff would appear later at the Ball when there were few adults watching!) and acting overly civilised.

The social network between the Edinburgh private schools is quite complex. For example, one company owns 3 of them: George Watson's College, Stewart's Melville College (SMC) and the Mary Erskine School for Girls (MES). But, on top of that, SMC and MES, whilst separate schools on separate locations, share the same Principle Teacher and some classes in the final year are mixed.

To complicate matters further, some of the boys' schools go on trips and holidays with some of the girls' schools.

The whole idea behind the Edinburgh private schools is to keep creating the next generation of the Capital's business community. That is why the Old School Tie network is so powerful and important in Edinburgh: the network has been building since a person's early childhood!

Elitist school life leads to elitist university life which, in turn, leads to elitist business life.

This is ultimately how Edinburgh operates. Quietly. Privately. Behind closed doors and between similar people of similar backgrounds.

What is important to note is that it is not about how much money a person has. Money alone will not buy you a place at these dinner parties. It is about your background, your upbringing, where you lived and the school you went to. Wealthy 'nouveau riche' types are rarely *really* admitted to the 'club'.

It might seem strange therefore that David Murray, an Ayrshire lad, would become so well-connected in the Edinburgh Establishment. As the son of a convicted (time-served) criminal, he seems an unlikely candidate for membership.

This is partly explained because Murray did attend Fettes College (where former Prime Minister Tony Blair was educated) in Edinburgh for a while and both of his sons attended a couple of Edinburgh private schools: firstly Daniel Stewart's and Melville College (now called Stewart's Melville College) and also Merchiston Castle School.

Fettes College

Stewart's Melville College

Merchiston Castle School

It is also partly explained by the fact that Murray moved to live in Edinburgh very early in his career. He lived in the right areas, like Murrayfield and Barnton and would have quickly established friendly contacts with neighbours who were part of the Edinburgh business community.

However, it was through clever use of his charisma, charm, wit and intelligence that he forged some key alliances with very well-connected Edinburgh people. For, whatever we may think of Murray, there is no questioning that he is a smart guy who has always been great at making smart friends!

This is how he developed his early business, Murray Metals, into the large multi-national and (for a while) successful Murray International Holdings he operates today.

The importance of having 'friendly' neighbours and sending your kids to private school should not be underestimated. As I mentioned above, the Edinburgh Establishment is a private, self-perpetuating, group of similar people.

This can be proved in a number of ways.

Firstly, the living arrangements of Scotland's 35 judges point to a caste far removed from those appearing before them in the dock. Although the Court of Session, which hears civil and appeal cases, is based in Edinburgh, the High Court, which hears the most serious criminal trials, moves around the country.

Yet approximately 83% of them live in Edinburgh, and 71% of them in just five posh Edinburgh postcodes: the New Town, the Grange, Murrayfield/Ravelston, Barnton/Cramond and Trinity. **Not a single judge lives in Glasgow, Dundee, Aberdeen or any other Scottish city.**

Scotland's 2nd richest neighbourhood consists of a handful of streets and just under 800 people, but they include no less than five judges. Lords Carloway, Kingarth, Turnbull, Uist and our old friend Lord Nimmo Smith all live within a few yards of each other in Murrayfield/Ravelston.

Secondly, a disproportionately large number of private school children go on to study law at university. A recent survey of the judges' schooling shows that they do have a similar upbringing, as well as similar tastes in property later in life. While only 4.5% of children in Scotland attend private schools, 71% of judges were educated in the private sector. A third attended either George Watson's College, Edinburgh Academy or Glenalmond in Perthshire.

Thirdly, sometimes the 'clubbishness' of the judiciary is quite literal. Membership of the exclusive New Club, a lynchpin of the Edinburgh establishment, appears *de rigeur* amongst judges, with 43% of them listed as members in Who's Who.

The New Club has always kept its secrets closely guarded behind its anonymous Princes Street doors.

It is treated as a home-from-home for Edinburgh's movers and shakers. What is interesting is that the club might seem like an old-fashioned edifice ... like something from the 19th Century but, in fact, it is still going strong. That is because it still offers the ultimate retreat and last word in discretion. Many members are related to those who joined from previous generations.

Of course it is not only the judiciary who were largely educated at private schools. I'm sure it won't surprise you to know that huge numbers of politicians and business leaders were privately educated too. According to a 2012 survey, 44% of leaders, businessmen and politicians were educated privately.

Even in sport the private school influence continues. Olympics 'dominated by privately educated'

Sir Chris Hoy attended the George Watson's College in Edinburgh. Indeed, a staggering 50% of TeamGB medallists at the Beijing Olympics came from private schools. Or, to put it another way, half of TeamGB's medals came from just 7% of the population. In addition to Hoy, Ben Ainslie and every single one of the equestrian medallists went to private schools.

Football is different, however. Around 7% of players come from private schools and this reflects the percentage of children across the whole of the UK who are privately educated.

Why is this? The answer is simple: money.

Private schools can usually afford to devote more time to sport, and have far better facilities and often top-class coaches. That is especially the case in sports where the basic cost of taking part is high, such as equestrian events and sailing.

It is also true that a disproportionate number of officers in the British Army were educated in private schools. This proportion is even greater when looking solely at the Scottish Regiments and there is a good reason for this.

For those who are unaware, many Edinburgh private schools have a cadet force (Army, Navy and Air Force) and many hundreds of pupils join up. In many ways, cadet forces can be written-off as fancy 'adventure camping' but it is a little more than that.

For starters, each child (for remember, they *are* still children) receive a uniform (depending on which force they join) and, in the case of the Army Cadets, they are officially affiliated to one of the Regiments, normally the Royal Scots.

Most significantly though is that fact that some of the schools have – on school premises - an armoury containing British Army weapons. Real guns! And the children are taught how to handle them, clean them, load them and use them.

There are regular weekend and week-long camps throughout the year when the children stay in genuine British Army bases and perform various activities, including live firing as well as some joint activities with regular army personnel.

It is no wonder that many Edinburgh private schools have links with Sandhurst and it is normal for a few pupils from these schools to apply to Sandhurst each year.

I have tried to give a flavour of life in the Edinburgh private schools. It is difficult because it really is a unique environment. But they key point of life in those schools is that their 'way' becomes normal. The rest of the city, the rest of Scotland, the rest of society doesn't really exist.

They aim to churn-out like-minded individuals who will all do their best to maintain the status quo and to preserve the elitism of the schools.

To preserve the Edinburgh Establishment.

Murray Loves The Green-(belt)

The Edinburgh Green Belt was officially designated as a continuous belt around the city in which construction developments were (largely) prohibited. It has essentially remained in place but with some interesting 'exceptions'.

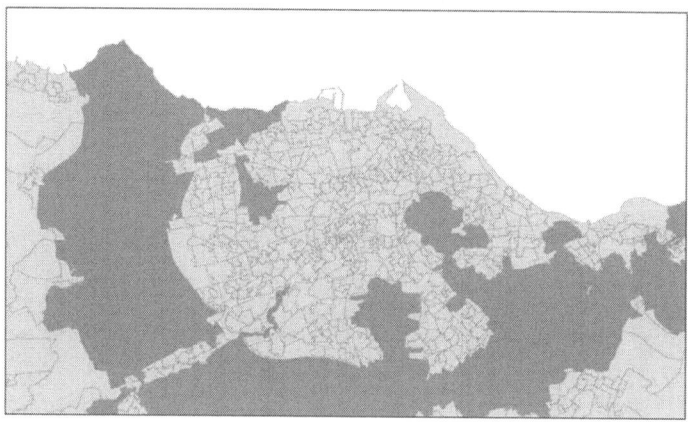

Edinburgh Green Belt

In the 1980s, David Murray bought hundreds of acres of land to the west of Edinburgh, within the Green Belt. The land was generally used for farming and, as such, did not cost him much money. It was cheap because it was in the Green Belt so could not be used for construction.

However, in the 90s there was a review of the planning laws relating to this land and, suddenly, huge tracts of it were useable for construction projects. Land that had once been farms was now shopping centres and office blocks.

There might also have been a football stadium there if Murray had had his way.

Before Romanov bought Hearts, Murray offered land at Hermiston Gait to them for the construction of a new stadium. This land would have had few problems receiving planning permission from the City of Edinburgh Council planners.

However, what is more interesting is that this was not the first time Murray offered land to Hearts for a new stadium. He offered to do the same thing when Wallace Mercer was still the owner.

Mercer, who incidentally lived in Barnton (and whose children were educated at the Mary Erskine School and Stewart's Melville College), initially tried to build a new stadium at Millerhill, to the east of the city, but then switched to the Hermiston Gait option. This was the option put fully to the City Council. However, the stadium was part of a larger development plan that included commercial buildings and houses.

In other words, the Murray/Mercer plan was to use the building of a football stadium as a smokescreen that would hide the really important part of the plan: the get around the strict Green Belt planning laws.

This is because exceptions could be made if there was a 'social benefit' created by the development. When the Council refused planning permission for the commercial developments, the stadium plan collapsed because the profit is generated for the owners/developers through those associated commercial and housing developments.

So Mercer's plan failed but Murray still made a fortune because of the subsequent change in the planning laws. Of course it was just good luck. Or was it?

Whilst there is no explicit proof that Murray directly influenced the change in the planning laws it does seem a remarkable coincidence that, just a few years after buying the land, the laws were changed. Why would he buy several hundred acres of land if it was to be unusable?

Perhaps we can ascertain a clue in a much more recent example of how cunning he can be.

In 2010, Murray earmarked a huge area of his land (land that was still in the Green Belt) for a 60-acre national garden complex. This is supposed to be Scotland's answer to the hugely successful Eden Project, in Cornwall and is part of a much larger construction project, including sports, education, commercial and housing developments, estimated to cost £1billion.

When he had this idea, he immediately had his lackeys in the media start mouthing-off the propaganda to 'sell' the idea to the public.

We were told that 650 jobs would be created in the Hermiston Gait area, close to the Gyle Shopping Centre and RBS's world headquarters (I'll come to RBS in a moment), as part of a 20-year plan.

The Calyx Project

The 25 million "Calyx", billed as a world-class horticultural visitor attraction, would boast a string of themed gardens, water features, educational facilities and research facilities. It was expected to attract half a million visitors a year and become one of Scotland's leading tourism attractions.

The sports village would feature a major arena capable of housing football, rugby and possible athletics events, while a national curling academy and several sports pitches would also feature. Edinburgh Rugby is already thought to be a contender to use the stadium. The stadium will be on the site that Hearts were interested in several years earlier.

Two new primary schools, a high school, community centres, shops and parks would also be built to serve three separate neighbourhoods which are envisaged as part of the development.

Murray owns 80% of the land needed for the development. But does he have the cash to pay for it? Of course not. The financial backing is coming from Murray's good friends at Lloyds Banking Group (I will also say more about them later!).

Perhaps I am just being cynical but it is interesting to note that, after their involvement in RFC and MIH, they are keen to 'support' his plan for such a massive development.

But, then again, if the development succeeds, Murray makes a fortune ... and he will no doubt be 'encouraged' to use some of that fortune to buy back the stake Lloyds own in MIH (I mention more about that later, too).

However, for it to get off the ground, it will need special permission from Edinburgh Council and the Scottish Government to go ahead and is likely to face opposition from environmental campaigners. But, as he has attempted in the past, Murray is using the 'social smokescreen' as a tool to make a killing. In other words, he believes the project's 'environmental credentials' and potential economic benefits will help sway the authorities.

So, how can he be so confident when there are clearly huge obstacles to be overcome?

As mentioned above, having good friends can always be useful.

Scotland's chief planner, Jim Mackinnon, accepted an invitation to give the opening speech at the project's official launch in which he praised it as an "exciting development".

The problem with a comment like that is that huge developments like this are usually subject to a public inquiry. In such an event, Mackinnon would likely play a key role in deciding whether or not the development gets the final go-ahead.

Mackinnon was invited by Murray to give the address at the event. The event was paid for by Murray. In his speech, he praised Murray's "passion and sincerity".

This is the same man who had private meetings with Donald Trump and his people before the decision was granted to allow Trump to build his Golf Country Club close to Aberdeen.

Is Murray just lucky? Does this merely have the whiff of a mega-casino about it or could it actually fly?

I am not saying that there is anything dirty going on with this man but do you feel confident that everything is above board?

I wonder what other friends Murray has 'helping' his business interests?

Murray International Holdings

For convenience, I shall not refer to Murray's different companies as they evolved over the years. I shall simply refer to MIH because there are certain consistencies relevant to all of his companies. Also, to save you from being overloaded with numbers and figures, I am focusing more on the financials of the recent past as that is when things have become much more interesting!

There are a few key areas of particular interest in the MIH Web shown below.

The first relates to David Murray Jnr ... the heir to the throne and his previous jobs with IMG (who own the SPL Media Rights) and the Bank of Scotland, who were so accommodating to MIH and Rangers FC. If we remember for a moment that Rangers FC was never supposed to die, that the Murray dynasty was meant to continue through David Jnr, then he would have found himself in the pleasant position of having worked for those 2 important organisations.

He would have been sitting in his office at Ibrox (well, probably Charlotte Square in Edinburgh, actually) and been dealing with various senior people at the Bank of Scotland. And, chances are, he would know them personally through his time working there.

I'm sure that, like me, you have no doubt that those discussions would have involved no favouritism as at all. No. None whatsoever.

He also worked for IMG who hold the media rights with the SFA. Again, I'm sure that having personal friendships with those involved would lead to no benefit whatsoever.

The second relates to the Bank of Scotland itself and how it, through its ownership of Uberior Investments, owned 12% of MIH and then Lloyds, in 2010, **doubled that investment to 24%.**

In fact, the Bank of Scotland increased its share-holding in MIH over the years. In other words, the bank increased its exposure to the financial performance of Murray and his empire.

If it all came crashing down, they would lose money. Did this affect their reasoning when dealing with him?

Of course, this is how it was *supposed* to be. Nobody knew that the global financial crisis would come along and essentially kill the 2 big Scottish banks. Nobody knew that the Bank of Scotland would be taken over by Lloyds ... an English bank run by English bankers who don't give a shit about the Edinburgh Establishment and Scotland's Establishment football club.

The most significant part of the MIH Spider's Web, is the large area filled by Sir Angus Grossart.

Sir Angus Grossart

According to the Scotland on Sunday newspaper, Sir Angus Grossart *"has a reputation for being Scottish businesses' primary fixer, with a finger in almost every meaningful pie in the Scottish economy"*.

He is chairman and executive director of Noble Grossart, the merchant bank he founded in 1969. Educated at Glasgow Academy and Glasgow University, he is an influential figure in the Scottish art world and he sits or has sat on the boards of (amongst others):

- Royal Bank of Scotland – Vice Chairman
- Edinburgh Fund Managers – Board Member
- Trinity Mirror – Board Member
- Hewden Stuart – Board Member
- Scottish Investment Trust – Boar Member
- National Galleries of Scotland - Chairman
- Scottish Opera – Vice President
- The Edinburgh Film Festival - Director
- National Museums of Scotland – Chairman
- Scottish Futures Trust – Chairman
- Lyon & Turnbull – Chairman
- Royal Scottish National Orchestra – Chairman
- Heritage Lottery Fund – Chairman
- The Fine Art Society – Chairman
- Noble Grossart Merchant Bank – Founder and Chairman
- British Petroleum – Board Member

- Scottish Enterprise – Director

- Scottish & Newcastle Brewers – Board Member

- Murray International Holdings – Board Member with 5.5% holding (now "cancelled")

This is the man who has been at Sir David Murray's side – and in his boardroom – for decades. There are few individuals in Scotland who can so readily be identified with the Establishment. This man had shared dinners and cocktails with every important mover and shaker in the land.

It is simply not possible to be on so many boards and trusts as him without having every connection available.

But perhaps he never used his connections when on the MIH Board. Perhaps he never mentioned MIH to anyone at the countless dinner parties he has attended over the decades. Perhaps Murray has obtained no benefit whatsoever from having this man standing by his side for so long.

Perhaps ...

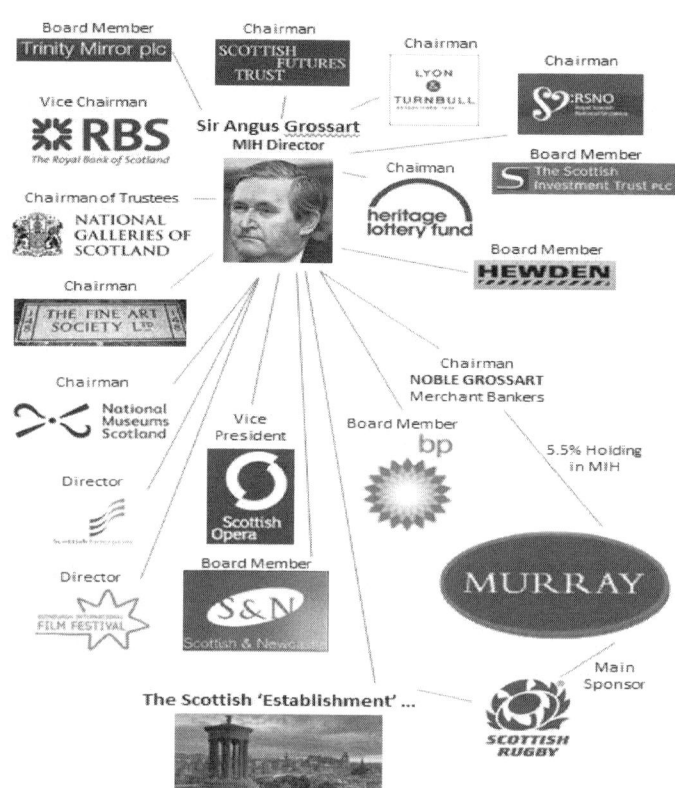

Rangers FC

In a similar to MIH, but to a lesser extent, Murray has also surrounded himself with well-connected people at Rangers. We all know these characters well by now and they require no further introduction. The best known of these connections is Campbell Ogilvie (did he ever really leave Rangers??) and his key position in Scottish football.

What is interesting to note, however, are the 'links' between Regan and Coors as well as the links between Murray Jnr and the Bank of Scotland and IMG.

Of course, I'm sure you're as confident as I am that these links are mere coincidences and have no tangible effect whatsoever on recent events ...

Financial Leniency leads to Financial Doping

So, it is clear that Murray has worked extremely hard at cultivating close links with well-connected individuals. But what was the intended purpose of those cultivated connections? What did he hope to gain from them?

Of course it is entirely possible that the outsider from Ayrshire simply wanted to 'belong'. Perhaps he merely longed to be a part of the Establishment and craved no further benefit from it.

It's possible. But is it likely?

Another possibility is that he wanted to benefit financially – and his companies to benefit financially – from having friends in the right places.

Let's have a little look at some of the key financial information in relation to Rangers FC and MIH and compare those figures to the treatment received by Celtic FC over the same period.

I don't want to turn this into a dull lesson in finance so I have kept it as simple as possible. The graphs shown below represent the results published in the Financial Statements of MIH, Rangers FC and Celtic FC as submitted to Companies House.

Chart 1, below, summarises the financial results of Rangers FC during the years 1988 to 2009. In this graph it is clear to see that Turnover (in red) increased steadily for the most part until experiencing some volatility from 2005.

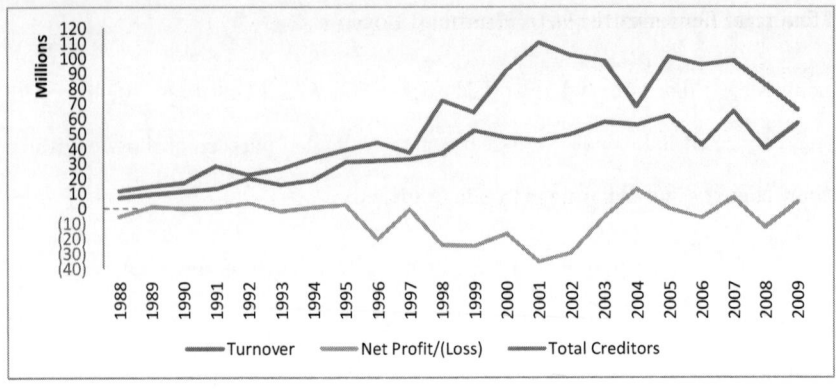

Chart 1: RFC Results 1988 to 2009

What is more interesting, however, is the clear correlation between Net Profit/(Loss) and Total Creditors (Total Creditors includes all amounts owed by the club, including bank debts and trade creditors etc). From the moment Murray first climbed the Marble Staircase, he was borrowing more money than the club earned. Creditors climbed steadily until 1997 when the figure started to increase dramatically. This figure peaked in 2001 when it reached approximately GBP110 million.

The sharp increase in creditors, in 1997, came shortly after the club started making regular net losses and, as the losses grew, the creditors grew too.

This is interesting because these early years were during Celtic's dark days of the 90s. Rangers won 9 championships in a row, were guaranteed Champions League money, and yet they still barely broke-even during all of this time. Indeed, their debt was building.

It's worth remembering that, during these years, Aberdeen FC (running on a shoestring budget) lost out on the Premier League Championship twice on the last day of the season.

I find these figures particularly interesting because we were all led to believe, during those times, that Murray was some sort of modern day King Midas and that his success was due to his unparalleled business acumen.

Chart 2, below, shows a little more detail as to what was going on at Rangers during those same years.

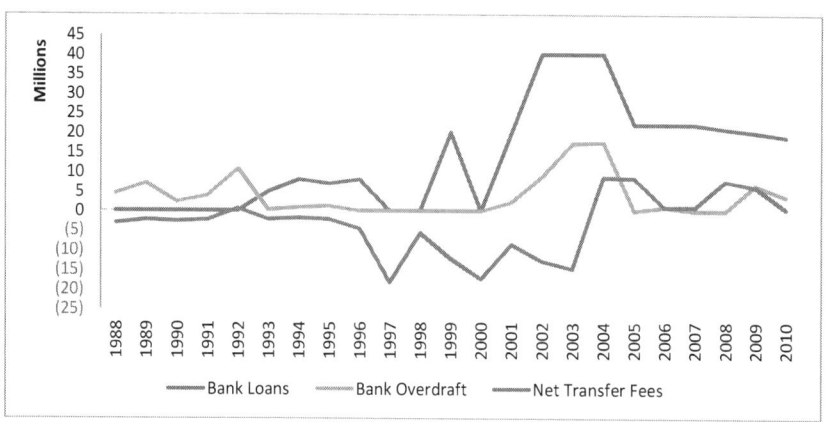

Chart 2: RFC Spending & Bank Support 1988 to 2010

Here we see that the club was almost always spending more on new players than it received from sales. There was one exception to this, in 1992, but this trend remained until 2004.

The chart also shows how generous the club's bankers were during this period. The bank overdraft peaked, between 2003 and 2004, at almost GBP17.5 million and the bank loan peaked, between 2002 and 2004, at GBP40 million.

Bear in mind that this bank generosity was during years when the club was consistently making net losses (see Chart 1).

But maybe the banks were being equally generous to the other big club in Scotland?

A comparison with Celtic FC

Chart 3, below, compares the Net Profit/(Loss) of Celtic FC and Rangers FC during the years 1993 to 2010.

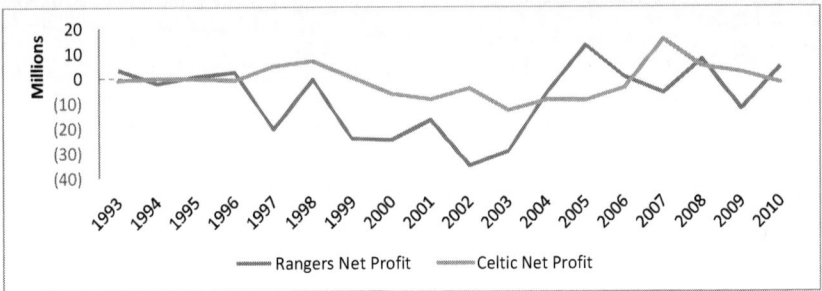

Chart 3: Celtic & Rangers Net Profit/(Loss) 1993 to 2010

This chart is striking in that it shows the dramatically different financial performances of the two club during those years. As can be seen, Rangers made significantly larger losses, peaking at GBP35 million in 2002, that Celtic. Celtic's worst financial result was a loss of GBP13 million in 2003.

Chart 4, below, compared the Total Creditors of the 2 clubs during the same period.

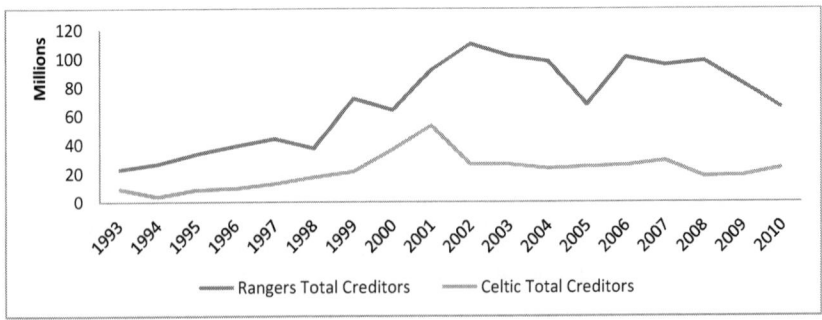

Chart 4: Celtic & Rangers Total Creditors 1993 to 2010

These figures show the total debts of both clubs. It is clear that Rangers FC enjoyed vastly greater debts, peaking at GBP100 million in 2002 compared to Celtic's peak debt of GBP53 million in 2001.

Chart 5, below, compared the Bank Support offered to the 2 clubs during those years.

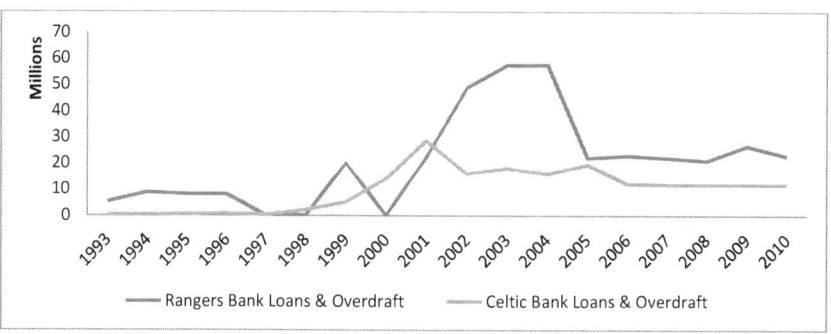

Chart 5: Celtic & Rangers Bank Support 1993 to 2010

These figures are even more astonishing in that they clearly demonstrate that Rangers enjoyed vastly higher bank loans than Celtic did during the same time.

The previous 3 charts show clearly the uneven financial playing field of those years. What has always amazed me is that in the early 90s, when Celtic was on the brink of destruction with the Bank of Scotland ready to pull the plug, our financial performance was still better than Rangers.

And yet, for year after year, Rangers were allowed to build up extortionate levels of debt. All supported by their bankers.

"Ah, but Celtic did not have a genius like David Murray running the club ... THAT is why the banks were so understanding". That is an excuse I heard many times from the media during those years.

So, let's have a look at some financial aspects of Murray International Holdings ... the main company of the 'genius'.

Chart 6 shows Turnover, Net Profit/(Loss) and Total Creditors of MIH during 1999 to 2012. We can see that the company has barely ever made a profit although it has made continuous net losses in recent years, peaking at GBP175 million in 2009.

What is more shocking, though, is the position relating to Total Creditors. These largely continued to grow until a peak of GBP1.08 billion (yes, **more than ONE THOUSAND MILLION pounds**) in 2009.

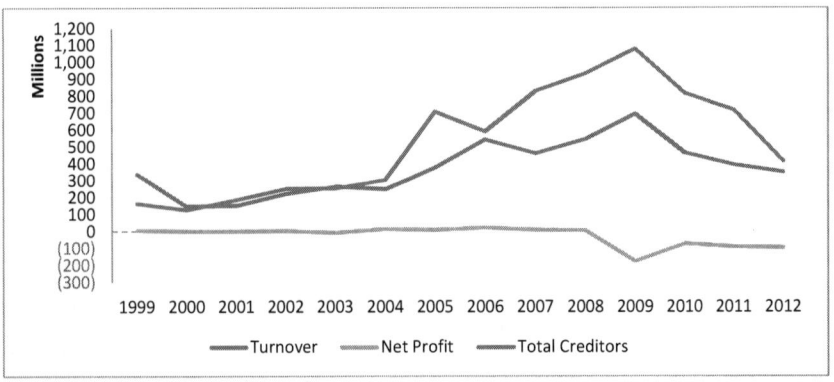

Chart 6: MIH Results 1999 to 2012

Within the Total Creditors figure are those for Bank Loans and Bank Overdrafts. These can be seen in more detail in Chart 7, below.

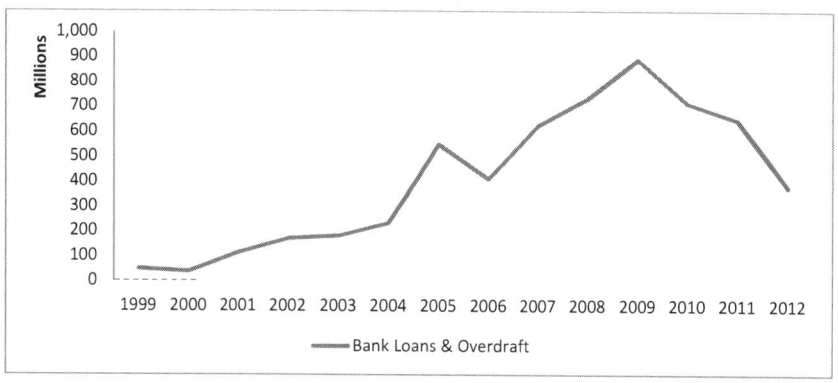

Chart 7: MIH Bank Support 1999 to 2012

Here we can see that, just as they were with Rangers FC, the MIH bankers have been very accommodating. Total bank support to MIH peaked at GBP889 million in 2009.

Lloyds PLC, Donald Muir & Financial Collapse

You may have noticed some substantial changes in the MIH figures shown in Charts 6 and 7, above, and specifically that those changes occurred around 2009.

This is no coincidence.

On 17 September 2008, very shortly after the demise of Lehman Brothers, HBOS's share price suffered wild fluctuations between 88p and 220p per share, which lost almost half its market value in the week, despite the Financial Services Authority's assurances as to its liquidity and exposure to the wider credit crunch.

However, on 18 September 2008 the terms of the recommended offer for HBOS by Lloyds TSB were announced. The two lenders also revealed plans to raise a combined £17 billion under a government-funded recapitalization programme aimed at strengthening the UK banking sector's capital reserves. The government backed the deal using a special national interest clause on the grounds that a collapse of HBOS would have had a disastrous impact on the UK.

On 16 January 2009 the Lloyds TSB acquisition of HBOS was completed following final court approval and Lloyds TSB was renamed Lloyds Banking Group plc.

Suddenly, facts and figures, decisions and strategy were all being discussed in London by the new rulers of the Bank of Scotland. No longer were Edinburgh friendships – forged in leafy suburbs during dinner parties – worth much. Lloyds really didn't care what school you went to or what Daddy does for a living.

But they weren't stupid either. They knew they couldn't just pull the plug on MIH/RFC. But they weren't buying Murray's nonsense so they needed somebody in those companies singing to their tune.

Donald Muir has the reputation of being a safe pair of hands, both among the lender community and his insolvency peers, racking up a string of successful turnarounds.

Of course, we know him best as a director of RFC and MIH. As the Lloyds go-to guy it seems that Muir was catapulted onto Rangers' board by the bank to keep an eye on its efforts to reduce its debt - with the majority of that debt owed to Lloyds.

Donald Muir joined the RFC Board and Lloyds became the Bankers of MIH in 2009. This was the reason for the dramatic shift in the debt dynamics at MIH and was the beginning of the end for the media-spun moonbeams.

Rangers subsequently reduced its debt from £33m to £18m, and Muir stepped down along with Lloyds on the day current owner Craig Whyte took over.

The Armageddon of Rangers

So who really had the power to allow Rangers FC so many years of unique treatment. Unique *financial* treatment.

The Daily Record? BBC Scotland?

Did organisations like that have enough influence to allow Rangers to stack-up such staggeringly enormous debts?

I don't believe so.

I believe that it was because Murray cultivated his connections with the Edinburgh Establishment that Rangers were allowed to get away with behaviour that no other club, not least Celtic, could get away with.

In my view, Murray quickly realised where the real power in Scotland lay and he used that to his advantage. It was only when the financial landscape changed after 2008 that he lost all of those advantages because that was when Edinburgh, and in particular its banks, suddenly lost its ability to live in its own little bubble.

Suddenly, decisions were being taken in London by people who didn't live in the same neighbourhoods and whose children didn't go to the same school. Suddenly, nobody cared who he was and who his friends were.

Suddenly, he had lost the Edinburgh Establishment.

And the rest, as they say, is history ...

What you just read is the whole of basis of *The Asterisk Years*. What you will, hopefully, now read is the story around it.

3-Self-Evident

There's room at the top they are telling you still,

But first you must learn how to smile as you kill,

If you want to be like the fool on the hill,

A working class hero is something to be.

A working class hero is something to be.

If you want to be a hero, well just follow me

A meeting with Downton Abbey

And that's that

So how did I get involved?

Well, there I was, writing this book one day when, building up to tear Lord Nimmo-Smith apart and all that, an email comes into me. At first, when I saw the name, I thought it a crank and even more so when I saw the subject matter "Good Evening", this is what it said:

"Good Evening Paul,

Sorry for disturbing you I got your email address from your blog.

On Friday November 22nd 1963, President John F Kennedy was assassinated in Dallas, Texas. Much has been written and theorised over who was ultimately responsible for his murder. Many believe it was Fidel Castro, or the Soviets, or the Mafia. Some even still believe it was plain old Lee Harvey Oswald acting alone.

There are countless murky details connected with that day but two, in particular, have always stood out to me. The first is that the route of his car journey was changed on the morning he arrived in Dallas. This new route included the slow, tight turn onto Elm Street outside the Texas School Book Depository. The second is that, again that morning, the decision was taken to remove the bullet-proof glass roof of his car.

Could Castro have made those decisions? Could the Soviets or the Mafia? Could Lee Harvey Oswald?

No.

Some decisions can only be made in private rooms, behind closed doors, between incredibly well-connected individuals. Those faceless people with **real** *power and influence.*

This brings me to our dear departed friends who once resided at 150 Edmiston Drive, Glasgow.

Much has been written about them. Much is still to be discovered and remarked upon. We have all heard about EBTs and how they allegedly cheated to win some titles and cups. Much has been written, and continues to be written as to whether those trophies should be erased from the history books.

But I would argue that the EBTs and whatever else is merely a side-show. To me, this is simply a distraction from the **real** *cheating and double-standards that allowed them to prosper and succeed for so long.*

The fact is that Rangers FC was Scotland's 'Establishment Club', with freedom for Murray to do as he pleased.

The media has often been portrayed as being at the centre of this conspiracy. The succulent lamb-munching tabloid 'journalists' and their brethren on radio and television are credited with allowing Murray and the Establishment Club to have a free (red?) hand to do anything.

But is the Glasgow-based media really so powerful? Given that they have been attacking Celtic so ferociously and for so long, and yet we are thriving and prospering, it suggests to me that they have no power. It seems to me that they are not the power itself but merely its mouthpiece.

Just as with JFK, it is the hidden forces that truly hold power. It is those faceless decision-makers who allowed Murray's ego, and empire, to flourish.

Those forces are not to be found in Glasgow. The real power in Scotland lies in Edinburgh and its incestuous private school/business fraternity. This is where Murray derived his grace and favour to do as he pleased with other people's money.

This is the Edinburgh Establishment."

I read it four times, looked at his email address, it checked out. I ran a check on the ISP and it was in continental Europe. I looked beyond the poor lesson in conspiracy and googled the guy. He was real, he exists. I've been in this position before and you have to be very careful. So I replied asking if he could send a picture of himself with a copy of today's newspaper.

Then I hit send.

I went back to writing but kept half an eye on my email. Amazingly, the reply came within ten minutes.

It had an attachment.

It was a picture of the guy holding up a copy of *The Economist* from two days before.

The reply said: "An internet bampot telling me to buy a newspaper-hahaha"

Alright ya cunt, calm yerself.

So we bounced emails back and forth until very late in the night, it was summer of 2012 and raining. Over the course of the next year we spoke a lot on Skype, emailed, talked on the phone, fell out, screamed at each other, almost lost contact and also met twice, once in Edinburgh in October 2012 and once in a secret European location in August 2013.

This book is the result of that.

This man would open my eyes into a world that had its guns trained on Celtic for two decades.

Too Big(oted) To Fail

It was a conversation with Graham Wilson that made me realise that my game needed to upped. It was the day before we were getting the trophy against St Johnstone in May 2013. He had told me about a rant he was going to do on *Beyond The Waves* and I listened to him and said that he should do it another day, we were getting the league trophy tomorrow and we should never take that for granted. He reflected and said I was right, that because he didn't live through the 90's with Celtic, he was taking things a wee bit for granted. It made me think as well though, were we now so far away from the 90's now that it was no longer a reference we could go back to? Were people aware of just what we were up against and did they know the extent of it? It's ok for me to spout it in pubs but were people acutely aware of just how much of an advantage had against us? And that's before we are talking about Referees or EBT's.

Strapping in.

Bob was an affable, amiable kind of guy. After we established a trust, we started to talk more and more. Not just about the stuff contained in the book but his interests (Vivaldi, Travel, books by P.G. Wodehouse), his views on current affairs (Thinks the EU is a good idea but run by halfwits, hates Gordon Brown, doesn't understand David Cameron) and the best places he has been (Brazil was fantastic, loves Bath and wants to finish his days in Switzerland)

Often he would talk at length about certain things and I'd go from thinking that I had a new mate to God this cunt is an establishment wanker.

It became clear to me from the get-go that the information he had was going to be hard for me to get my head round and also, like a lot of sources, they sometimes don't realise that some bit of information they have, some minutiae, can be huge for other people. After he dropped a few hints and I told him one night on a Skype Video Call that I had intended to write a book about EBT's and the real victims, perhaps he could help?

He paused for so long that I thought the screen was frozen.

Then he cracked a smile and said "I've got to say something, I love all the stuff you guys do but you're all a bunch of naive bastards"

Not the answer I was expecting if truth be told.

Bob went on to explain that although Rangers were no more, if anyone thought a combination of Craig Whyte and unpaid taxes took them down, they were sadly mistaken.

"Mate, this thing stretches far and wide and went into every part of Scottish society, they controlled everything"

Who is they?

"Murray and cohorts. Well, Murray really. With the intention of his son taking over in due course"

I stopped him there. There was a huge temptation to leap up, run to my window, open it and shout "I FUCKING TOLD YOU SO!!!" until I collapsed but I'm older now and I know how journalists scoff at information, I know how stories get buried in a thousand tweets and I know how Rangers, and now Sevco fans, would just put this down as "another paranoid Tim" So I said to Bob that why I was ready to believe, I had no interest in writing a book about the collapse of Rangers and I also had be able to "sell" the story to the folk interested in my stuff and so there had to be tons of detail.

Again he smiled

"I worked in banks with millions of pounds for decades, detail is my forte"

Cool, but although we are obviously a part of this story, how much does it really have to do with us?

He looked at me incredulous as he sat on my lap (Skype remember...) and said:

"Paul, they had two goals, put Rangers at the top of European football and kill Celtic"

Never The Twain

Bob had been born in Edinburgh and worked within, what I'll call, the Axis of Evil, for many years. He had all the trappings of a comfortable lifestyle that first his parents provided then his private education would lead him on to. He got a job with a bank when he was 24 after attending the best schools Edinburgh could provide and then going to Cambridge. Among the many people he met at Cambridge, one friend he still remains in touch with to this day is Stephen Fry and indeed went to see him in Africa last summer. He lived in Edinburgh for many years, after coming back from Cambridge, in Cramond which has a picture in the dictionary when you look up the word "Plush". His job took him round the world often and afford him every luxury travel can give you. He always travelled business class, always stayed in the best hotels and has a confident air about him that you see in certain celebrities and sports stars where they just seem to effortlessly glide through life.

He had a good build for a man of his age (never asked but would guess late 50's) and after one tormenting afternoon it finally clicked and I realised that he was a ringer for Windsor Davies.

He had the air of a military man about him ("Don't be daft, private school helps you avoid all that nonsense") but with the glint of a man who enjoys a laugh and has a bit of madness in him. He likes a cigar ("Tribute to Wodehouse") and loves his wine but still partial to a pint now and again. He plays Badminton to stay fit ("Squash got too competitive") and has two sons, both of whom now live in New York, ("working in Wall Street, different types of jobs")

I should say at this point that I have never met anyone like Bob. I've met a few folk with money, mostly in New York and mostly obnoxious and unable to cope with it gracefully but Bob was different. He was charming and great to talk to (Most of the time) and had time for people.

I often wondered if he had every met anyone like me or indeed knew the area that I lived in about 1.5 miles from his house when he lived in Cramond.

He didn't conduct himself like anyone I knew, he always seemed happy and nothing ever seemed to be a problem for him. He was a straight-talker and didn't like bullshit (This would lead to our relations being strained at times when he argued about the importance of information).

As the summer of 2012 started to fade into autumn, I kind of went off message. I had the *By Any Means Necessary* book and launch were fast approaching and was full into education as well.

I also wasn't sure how to frame a book like this and had committed myself to *The Last Pearl Diver* coming out in March 2013.

I suppose if this book was going to ever fall apart then October 2012 would have been when it happened.

Then Bob said he was coming to Edinburgh.

I didn't know what to think at first. We had been talking to each other for about three months at this point and I got a bit nervous. Like I would with anyone, I offered him residence when he would be over here. Now, I don't live in a palace and I am surrounded by people who The Mafia pay protection money to so I thought he would politely decline and I'd breathe a sigh of relief and look forward to chatting in the bar of some luxury hotel in the centre of Edinburgh or maybe Malmaison down at the shore. Aye that would do me like.

So I did the polite thing and offered and the fucker jumped at the chance.

Oh Christ.

He gave me three days' notice as well and so, after college that day, I raced up to Home Base and bought paint and curtains for the Bedroom Tax room and got to work immediately.

I had become that guy who is always ten feet in front of The Queen.

The other thing I had constantly asked myself was "Why?" Why was this guy telling me all this stuff? What was in it for him?

I knew he took an interest in Celtic and was on Twitter, Facebook, listened to the podcasts and was completely dialled in to people like Phil Mac Giolla Bhain, Paul Brennan and Matt McGlone but he never really mentioned Celtic that often and didn't seem to come from a world where Celtic would be the love of your life, quite the opposite in fact.

So, the day before he flew over and we would meet for the first time, we had an email marathon and I asked him why, I said I got that he was a Tim and all that, by why was he telling me all this?

His reply came an instant after I had pressed clicked on send.

"They're a bunch of cunts mate"

Frost/Nixon

Bob was flying-in on a Friday. I said I'd come and meet him at the airport and he said "I thought you didn't drive?" then poured scorn on me for my suggestion that I waste time and money coming out on the airport bus to meet him. His words.

I suggested we meet in a bar on St Johns Rd, The Centurion. It was a little joke on my behalf, I'd used the pub for years to get my bus to Celtic games and thought this great meeting of minds should have a historical location. The fact it was on the road in from the airport and close to where I'd get off the bus was purely coincidental.

I hadn't been in The Centurion for many years and thought it was a good place to meet as it was always populated by cunts from Corstorphine who love their *Lyle and Scott*.

Upon arrival in the pub, I knew this was no longer the case. It was 4.30pm on a Friday afternoon but it felt like 2.30am on a Sunday morning.

Most of the punters in there had clearly been drinking all day. I call them punters as everyone in there seemed to have a bet on and were screaming profusely at the horses on the TV screen. I am well used to this kind of behaviour and have encountered folk like this on thousands of occasions.

Just never in The Centurion.

I went to the bar, got myself a Guinness and then took the seat nearest the window so I could hopefully see Bob as he appeared. I was just at the point when I wondered if he had landed yet (I'm always early) when a text came through asking if I was in the bar or lounge.

This guy knew his stuff.

Before I could text back "Bar" he appeared in my line of vision, coming round the corner like a golfer striding towards the 18th at the end of a great round and had a huge grin on his face as he spotted me immediately. He came in, dumped his bag and we hugged. It was a weird feeling meeting him and, thankfully, he seemed totally oblivious to the rest of the bar which I was convinced was ten minutes from wheeling out a bucking bronco.

I asked him what he wanted to drink and he flashed another big smile and said "I'll have what you're having"

His attire suggested he was made for The Centurion. Just The Centurion as I remembered it. I made my way to the bar and stood there for about seven minutes. Every so often I'd look over at Bob and give that look that says "Where is the fucking barman!!!" and he would chortle back.

Eventually this lazy prick appeared behind the bar and said "Oh, were you wanting something?"

Naw, I just love staring at the optics.

I took Bob's Guinness over and another for myself. We spent the next two hours chatting and drinking but the noise in the bar was reaching woman scorned levels so we decanted to an Italian restaurant nearby. It's the one next to the chippy and I'd never been in it in my life before and won't again (It was awful).

After we had ordered our food and had our Peronis put in front of us, I mentioned the book for the first time, I told him my fears about whether there was a book in this and if it was still relevant.

Bob knew exactly what I meant and said "Mate, I like you, you're a passionate guy but you doubt yourself too much. Listen, I'm going to lay out the whole story for you. Facts, figures, names, places. I'll out a lot of big-hitters and tell you stuff that will make people realise it's all true, every last word. Just don't name me in the book and never tell anyone it was me who told you all this"

I nodded. I'm a sucker for flattery (that was flattery, aye?)

I needed one thing though, I needed him to explain this to me face to face.

So in a shitty Italian restaurant in Corstorphine, half a mile from where the fuckers who tried to kill Celtic all lived, he did.

That's when I knew I had a book.

Cribs

By the time we got back to my flat, we were both fairly pissed. I was glad of that as I hoped it would make Bob miss the feint air of piss that frequently frequents my block.

We got in to my empty flat and I got two cans of Budweiser from the fridge. Bob planked himself on one of the couches (John Prescott was two jags, I am two couches, one a gimme and one I bought second hand for £60).

It became obvious really quickly that Bob couldn't give a toss about his surroundings. He was happy, pissed and great company.

I'm not sure he had a fucking clue where he was though. I sprung for a taxi (17 bastarding quid) and I was positive that he was totally oblivious to the fact that we could have walked to his old gaff in about 15 minutes (let me clarify this, I'm not rich, don't have a nice house, don't live in a perceived good area but do live really close to a perceived very good area, right on the cusp. In fact, years ago, there used to be a huge gate that separated the border if you will and recently one set of residents started a campaign to get the gate back. I'll let you guess which set).

At least, that's what I thought.

After shooting the breeze about all sorts of shit he said to me "I didn't realise you had property so close to the Murrays, old chap?" in a mock Downton Abbey type accent. I laughed and took him to mean Essex Road in Barnton. I knew Murray had a house there for years and I may have had knowledge of an incident where a flag was placed in his garden after a Celtic championship win plus I knew Wallace Mercer had a house there when he attempted to kill Hibs as I had heard stories of his kids, Helen and Iain, being taken to school from there, during the attempt, by armed guards.

So I mentioned Essex Road and he said "Oh yeah there, I was in that house many times"

That made me sit up.

I'd been in cars that had driven past Essex Road on many occasions, almost always after Celtic games and had often thought of the proximity (from Essex Road, I reckon you could be at my house, in a car, in under five minutes) as we had zoomed past it.

Throw in the Mercer connection and it was pretty much the start of hell as far as I was concerned. But no, I was wrong.

"I meant the one up the road there?"

What the fuck was Bob talking about? We had a fair bit to drink by this time but I tried to re-focus myself a bit and not give the game away that I had no idea what he was talking about.

I stuttered and stammered and eventually said "Which one?"

Bob looked at me as if I was taking the piss and said "Marchfield Park?"

Marchfield Park meant nothing to me. He would have been as well saying fucking Gosford Park to me.

"It's about a five minute walk from here?"

Once I'd established Bob wasn't taking the piss and I had slept off the drink and subsequent hangover, I let Bob sleep whilst I sparked up the laptop took to Google

Maps and confirmed that Marchfield Park was indeed a five minute walk away. I popped my head into Bob's room and I told him I was off out for rolls.

Of course I was really heading to Marchfield Park.

Marchfield Park is a private road that is off Queensferry Road in Blackhall, Edinburgh. It has huge gates in front of the four houses I saw in it (love a gate these posh cunts) and if you're reading this and thinking "I think I'll Google Earth that right now" don't bother, you'll get as far as the start of the street and no further. It is a brisk five minute walk from my house. All the years I lived in the area and I hadn't a clue. Plus I didn't know David Murray lived there either.

He did though, I checked.

This confirmed to me that I had to write this book, put everything I could into getting this story out there and try to make up for the fact that I could have tanned his windaes every night.

It also confirmed that Bob knew his stuff.

Dolly the Sheep

When I have written books previous to this one, it's normally just a lot of madcap tales that, at best, 1000 folk will read. This was different though. I felt a certain responsibility this time. Luckily I had a lot of inspiration. Men like Fergus McCann, Tommy Burns, Martin O'Neill and Neil Lennon refused to be part of that world. Men whose commitment to the cause made them a serious threat to the establishment that probably only Fergus knew existed but who would all feel its wrath over the course of their lives. If anything, it made them all the more determined to succeed.

Which is how it should be.

The Edinburgh Establishment ended up failing. Death by a thousand *cunts* if you will. The men named in this chapter are a big reason why that happened. You see, these business types thought that their true enemy would reveal themselves in the shape of a CEO with a corporate "grease the pole and succeed" background. They never reckoned on a wee guy from Croy who made it in Canada and had no business background in Scotland that they could influence. They didn't realise that Tommy Burns would begin the creation of a modern day Celtic that was a Jim Farry pen stroke away from stopping Rangers at eight in a row. Nor did they ever think a wee guy from Derry would obliterate Rangers most expensive ever team in one season and they certainly can't shake that thorn in the side that is Neil Lennon.

The other reason that the Edinburgh Establishment failed was because they were the establishment. See, friendly bank managers and inexhaustible overdrafts were never available to Celtic but they were the norm for people like David Murray. Our charts show how many pies he, and his right hand man Angus Grossart, had their fingers in. Forget EBT's, they were a mere sideshow. Rangers were able to use friendly bank managers and inexhaustible overdrafts to prop up a business that Celtic had long since wiped out. Liquidation would have taken place many years ago were it not for the establishment "piggy bank" that David Murray was able to dip into any time he felt like it and a network of like-minded old school tie pals ready to ask how old grannies all over Scotland were.

In June 2013, I had a walk around Murrayfield and surrounding areas. Tree-lined streets, huge houses, no noise apart from the hum of an odd lawnmower or a purring engine pulling into a long driveway. There weren't any gangs of kids, no "hoodies" except on the beautiful girls who were jogging and cycling round the various parks. The bikes were also very expensive and not bought from Sports Direct. The parks were all clean and the people in them looked tanned and healthy. This was a world I don't know or, at least, didn't know until now. I've seen plenty people in my life who have pretended to be rich and loads more who thought they were happy but how much money you have and how happy you are doesn't come into the life of The Edinburgh Establishment. What matters is power. If you take the street that both David Murray and Graeme Souness lived in, Easter Belmont Road in Murrayfield (Don't bother trying to have a look at it on Google Earth, you'll get as far as the start of the street), there was another famous inhabitant in the late 80's and early 90's. This inhabitant was *nouveau riche* and when he took location amongst The Edinburgh Establishment, he thought the ability to throw money around would guarantee him anything he fancied as this had always been the case previously. If you do Google Easter Belmont Road, you'll notice that it backs on to Murrayfield Golf Club.

Murrayfield Golf Club is not a typical golf club. The Clubhouse has a cosy old-fashioned feel to it with a large dining area and a really comfortable lounge area with thick carpets and country-house style sofas and armchairs to relax in. Imagine some fancy country estate: the interior is done up like that. Traditional looking but certainly not looking like it needs done-up. It's always in great condition, just like the course. The changing rooms are nice and clean with wooden lockers and there's a small pro shop on the side of the building.

The Club itself has an instant anomaly in that it has always had lady members, so it's not your typical misogynistic place. And there is a large junior section (fuelled mostly from the pupils of Daniel Stuart's plus the girls' schools of St George's and the Mary Erskine School). Sundays are always busy days as you get lots of families going for lunch. It would be normal to mostly see familiar faces and the vast majority of the kids went to private schools, of course, but it's a classic posh Golf club in that no jeans are allowed in the Clubhouse and the officials like to wear the club blazer or jumper as often as possible. It's very strict on membership, second only to the Royal Burgess Golfing Society of Edinburgh, so potential members would need to be sponsored by current members and that was never any guarantee of success although it is slightly more open now than it was than, say, in 1989.

So when Maurice Johnston tried to join, they told him to fuck off.

The Edinburgh Establishment is a closed shop and don't forget it.

That's the real extent of what Celtic were up against. We have shown you an insight in this book and *By Any Means Necessary*, of how it works at the SFA regarding all aspects of refereeing and now we have shown you how it worked, against us, for over two decades in Scotland.

You can be proud that you were not part of any of it.

Oh, and Dolly the Sheep, sponsored with Royal Bank of Scotland money and now sitting in the National Museum of Scotland in Chambers Street, Edinburgh, now who do we know with huge connections to both...

Prologue-

The Asterisk Years 2.0

When Murray shuddered at the Merchant City

So this book came out in October 2013. When I woke up on Saturday morning of the launch I realised I wasn't stressed at all about it. This was the first time that's ever happened to me on the day of a Book Launch so I am the type to think, even at that, something is bound to go wrong.

The 9.45am train from Haymarket pulled out from a sunny Edinburgh and powered into a dreech central belt that would set the weather tone for the day.

By the time I hit Glasgow, the rain was torrential, so what better way to spend the next hour than standing on grass in the open air. A tiny sacrifice given we were stood in front of the newly sculpted Celtic Cross that now stands in Dalbeth Cemetery as a monument to our founding fathers. Was good to bump into a few friendly faces like Stevie Cairney, Jason Higgins, Arthur Rusk and John Paul Taylor.

Umbrella sellers had a field day.

The game that day was a 1-1 draw versus Dundee Utd. It was damp, dull but we were still undefeated. As usual.

Straight after the game I met the Dublin Brigade of Conor, Mick and Darren and we made our way to the Merchant City.

This is the worst part of any Book Launch day for me, the bit where I am heading to it, it's all in front of me, everyone is looking forward to the craic and getting leathered into the drink and you're thinking "Fuck, it's me they are coming to see" The other aspect is it always nags at the back of your mind that this will be the time that no one shows up, it's pishing down, crap game, they will all go home. Thankfully when we got to Blackfriars, via The Libertine, several folk were already waiting outside the venue including the inimitable Richard Swan who is as much a part of these things as I am.

When I first got downstairs there were maybe around 40 folk there. Colette and her team had arrived and Richard whisked me away to the toilet to interview me, honest, we're just friends.

When I came out the entire place was packed and full of friendly faces. As well as the Dublin Brigade, my friend Paul had flown over for it and he has been a tower of strength to me for many years and I want to thank him now for always being there.

Similarly seeing folk like Simmy and Michelle again, always does my heart proud.

These nights would not be the same without Paul Lee and the wee man was there in his usual fine form and singing voice that Susan Boyle couldn't rival.

Always great meeting new friends like Hutchie, Eddie and David Brown.

The rain soaked and welcomed faced Hugh Clark even made an appearance, before he overthrows the SFA.

The people that come to these things are fantastic, I would say that wouldn't I, but these same people came to The Admiral in April 2012 and stood around wondering who everyone else was, 18 months on and they have drank together, sang together and, aye, even shagged each other some of them, and they are the heartbeat of these nights.

Krys Kujawa was first up and read some stuff from a new book he is doing and it was very well received. The bar had done us a real turn having a proper set up of chairs and stage for a night like this. Our host for this evening, the tasty Jo Laing (that will set off her radar) humbled me with her intro and before I knew it I was in front of the bright lights (An in joke for folk who were there).

What followed was a 90 minute show where I told the background to the book, illustrated the level of cheating we faced then took questions, heckles and incoherent rambling from the floor. In all seriousness it was great and really added to the night with a good toing and froing.

Blink and it was all over and Stevie Dodds led the illicit chanting and it has to be said, he was absolutely phenomenal. The raffle draw came and the lovely Louise Lavery won and ensured everyone knew about it. After that it was great to meet folk, catch up with friends, sign books and canoodle with Jane Hamilton.

Plus everyone who came, listened, asked questions, sang and drank, the people on Twitter who wished me well and the people in the book group who continue to inspire you restored my faith in humanity, I'll never forget that.

Then it was over.

Not before though the 150 people who packed the pub sent David Murray and co a clear message that not only are we not sitting at the back of the bus any more, we are driving it head on towards you all.

This would be start. There was no going back now.

Fear and Loathing on the Murray trail

It wasn't a good few weeks for me or some people close to me after the book launch. On a personal level my youngest son was very ill. Concerns about my own health were ongoing and the usual shit life throws at you all added to a worrying time.

It was all so different the week before when I bounced out of Ireland after a great gig in Larne. Soon as I got back though a shit-storm was brewing. Seems there had been threats made about the publication of a video of the Glasgow launch of *The Asterisk Years*. Not to me directly but to people close to me. I realised then that things were getting wee bit sinister as only three people even knew about the video and I was one of them. I knew the other two were solid so it was clear dark forces were raging. Not the type like the serial abuser who bombarded me, Amazon and Lulu with abuse, not even the coward who threatened my eldest son, no, this was the type who tried three weeks before it to get the book shelved completely.

I took the decision to pull the plug on the video, to protect others or at least, hopefully, stop them being threatened. You see I never get threats to my face, they always come on social media or through other people, but it didn't derail the project

The people who abuse and make threats, from your own side or the other, all have one thing in common. They are all saying "PEOPLE LIKE YOU ARE NOT SUPPOSED TO HAVE AN OPINION"

We said back "WE HAVE ONLY JUST BEGUN"

Balls

I've also wanted the balls to look at something and say "I can do that". You know like when Yosser Hughes follows the guy lining the football pitch in *Boys From The Black Stuff*. "Oh yeah, too right I can" That swagger that so many of the working class have worn out of them laced with the desperation to feel useful again. The sort that answers the question "What are the Shetlands like?" with "It's cold and full of ponies". I've been like that a lot of my life but have had confidence chipped away and paranoia chip in enough times now not to dive into anything feet first anymore. "Go on, giz it". Just to stand up to the fucking establishment and be like that.

It was in conversations on Facebook that The Asterisk Years Project really started. This flood of information that came my way which would became a book, an audio book and even a documentary. Kind of. Funny thing is, that avenue ended on Facebook too. I'll come to that later. Originally the book was to be about Lord Nimmo-Smith's "Punishment" of Rangers after finding them guilty of a decade of cheating. I had no idea then I would end up knowing his street as well as I do my own. Not that I did anything illegal there, but I had to see for myself just how close geographically he was to David Murray. That's who the story ended up being about of course, Minty, but then if you are reading this, you probably know that. Once the book took a different trajectory, it became a much harder write. I knew there wasn't enough information at that time to fill an entire book so I decided to run it alongside some of my own experiences as a sort of contrast piece. This would become where the main area of abuse would stem from. I get a lot of praise for these stories but the main venom I get directed at me is from people who absolutely loathe them. I think it's part snobbery, part jealousy, part constructive. I was privileged to discuss this with David Peace for 20 minutes one night. I think his most recent book, *Red or*

Dead, is a masterpiece, yet he told me about some of the comments he got from people and one night I sat going through all his one star reviews on Amazon and was stunned to read that there were so many and that a lot mirrored the sort of stuff I get. Not that I am comparing myself to him, baldy heids, black rimmed glasses and left wing leanings are about as much as we have in common but it opened my eyes. I know some people who hate me have written horrific things on reviews, I know that some of our friends from Ibrox have written some awful stuff to stop folk buying anything I do but I also now know some folk will just think it's shite. After all, if there are so many people telling David Peace he's shite, then I am going to get it in spades. I guess what I am saying is I've learned to separate the haters from the 'I hate this' folk.

Anyway, the idea of some personal background was to show that I lived a mile and a half from the Edinburgh Establishment but was a million miles from the opportunities they just love to bestow on each other. I drew on my own experiences growing up to try and show how they get away with it; namely that we don't know the opportunities exist therefore we can't get angry about them. I also needed a bit of transition. My previous books were a sort of punk fanzine style, I couldn't just go from that to presenting myself as a modern day Roger Cook without some sort of journey. Many writers inspire me, none more so than Brendan Behan, Irvine Welsh, Charles Bukowski and William Burroughs, but my other inspiration when writing was something I've never talked about before really. *Sniffin' Glue* was a fanzine for punks that my mate Drew had every issue of and I used to read a lot. Then when I moved to New York and made some money I started buying back issues and the inspiration hit again. It's a fantastic, balls out, fanzine, in the style that most fanzines have long since forgot and for folk like me it was a God send. The image here is the most inspiring thing I've ever seen. Here's three chords, now fuck off and start a band. Now, you know I don't do anything conventionally, so I wrote books.

I've grown to realise that my judgement has been clouded by that way of watching Celtic. Some people cannot relate to it and others recoil at the mere mention of it. That is increased ten-fold when I talk about poverty, alienation and desperation. I had noticed that any time I spoke about these issues on a blog or podcast the hate would spew towards me. I was a "Ned", a "Tramp", a "Casual" (Yeah, I know) and a "Schemie cunt". I was an embarrassment to Celtic and to all the great writers who have written about the club. Funny thing is, the books Celtic sell in the shop were partly the reason I started writing; not that I am against them just that they are, in the main, not to my taste. I wish them no ill will and indeed know and like very much a lot of the authors who are in there but it has to be said that not many of them jump in the trenches with me when the flak is flying towards me. No matter what I have done for them in the past.

Thing is, I have a kind of constant sniping in my ear because people cannot wait to tell you something bad. It's why I salute any Celtic supporter who puts their head above the parapet because I know what you'll face. I get poisonous reviews, horrible things said about me, tons of lies made up about me and lots of threats. Unfortunately, you get used to them. That's vile. No one should have to put up with that save for the one or two masochists out there who seem to need abuse like the bunny needs its Duracell. All this sounds awful doesn't it? Often I get asked, why do you bother? That's because they only see the bad side. Or at least what they think is the bad side. The real bad side is the breakdown of my marriage, a marriage that meant the world to me, because of who I was. The real bad side is not living with any of my sons. The real bad side is having Post Traumatic Stress Disorder that means I need to take five pills a day so I don't go off the reservation permanently. Those are what really worry me. I don't feel fear of things that normal people do. That's a curse because it means never backing down and sometimes you just need to let go. Just not on this.

The good side is the support. The book launches where you show off your work and pray people buy it and like it. It's the characters you encounter who help shape your next books. The ones who take the time to see how you are doing, boy, would they become important when the book came out. It's the people who have your back, a quality in life that is disappearing. They are the ones who never ask a question, never say "Why?", they just assure you that when the chips are down, they will flip em back up. I have a few of those people in my life, from ordinary, decent citizens to ordinary, decent criminals and even the odd extraordinary indecent woman. I decided after *The Asterisk Years* that it would be the last kind of book that I would do where I'd be revealing the most intimate aspects of my life. This book you are reading is written entirely by me so, technically, I've cheated a little bit, not to the extent of Rangers like, more Legia Warsaw. I thought I'd throw this diary in at the end of the project for anyone who was interested in the back story of *The Asterisk Years*, a story that would see me in a safe house for two days after a serious threat of my house being blown up, a story that exposed enemies that I previously thought were friends, a story where I would eventually enlist the help of a few pals who just happen to be La Cosa Nostra and a story that would take me right to the heart of the Edinburgh Establishment.

Balls out

The summer of 2013 was an awful time for me as I was writing this book. The book itself and pouring a lot of stuff into it was my way out. I spent a lot of time in and out of hospital after concerns were raised over my heart and kidneys. Essentially the effects of PTSD and a few genetic things had caught up with me but they did not know that then and I went through a worrying time of tests. At the same time I had to go to central Europe to meet Bob, the first main source, and sign off on the book. This meant a week sitting on Ryanair and bouncing round Ireland, Germany, France and Belgium. All this came at time when the hospital were in touch with more impending doom phone calls and letters, I wasn't drinking, but actually started smoking again, one of the worst possible things I could do, such was the worry I was going through at the time. I actually spent a week in Dublin and didn't touch a drop of the black stuff either. That week also pushed my mental stage to the brink. I'd gone over to meet my youngest son, Jake, and in that scenario all you do is look forward to it. However, a point comes in that time when the countdown is on to him leaving. We'd gone to Dublin Zoo and had a great time, various toy shops and all the stuff he likes. It was only from the Monday to the Wednesday and by the Wednesday morning I was not in the best form. I said goodbye to him at Connolly Station and broke down right there and then. Something inside me just snapped. I was off to meet friends for the rest of the week but my heart wasn't in it. The pressure of the book, my health issues and not being able to see Jake when I wanted had finally told and I spent two days crying my eyes out. A nervous breakdown it's called. I watched us beat Liverpool and went home the following day. Just before I got home I went to a local shop and bought 20 fags. I smoked them all in three hours.

I had to get my act together.

The following week was time to go to central Europe and meet Bob, ensuring he was all good with the book. It was a harrowing time, whilst being a fantastic host, Bob had many concerns about the information he had relayed and admitted he had many sleepless nights over it. This wasn't what I wanted to hear. We had a few heated debates and I finally agreed to take some stuff out. He was right of course, the more salacious stuff wasn't needed. I have to say as well, it's a lot easier having an argument in a £2m house than a council flat. Of course, when the British Establishment paedophile scandal broke, you could say that I regretted my decision to not pursue certain areas of investigation. It was a really good trip though and I knew then that the book was a goer, I didn't up until then, and so by late August, it was finished and ready to go to Harper to do the formatting required to make it book ready. Problem was Harper was going to New York on holiday and this wouldn't have been an issue had it not been for the new things I was trying. We had graphs in the book, these would be the bane of Harper's life for a while. We also had Q codes in them so folk could access stuff via their smart phone and I was pretty excited by that. I'd never seen it in a book before and saw it as a big step forward. At the time of writing, not a single person has even mentioned to me. You can't win em all.

As we moved into September, people started talking about the book, some in a "I can't wait" way and others in a "Oh that's the book about the Edinburgh Masons" type way. That was something I'd never had before, people telling me what was in the book before it was even out. Of course it was all wrong but for some reason they were utterly convinced by it. I then did an interview with Graham Wilson on *Beyond The Waves* and I can honestly say that my life has never been the same since.

Suddenly a lot more people were aware of me. A lot from the dark side who responded in their usual way but far outweighing the threats and abuse, came the adulation. My Twitter followers rocketed, invites to things started coming in and a lot of people started treating me differently. I started getting recognised at Celtic games and lots of people not only ask my opinion on things but also value it. Many, many people wanted to meet me before a game to get books signed or just have a chat, and some even wanted photos with my ugly mug in it. Gary Bergin in Larne got in touch and would start a trend that hasn't stopped. He invited me to launch the book in the north of Ireland, he'd put me up and the bar would fly me over. Someone was paying me to fly to them. I was so delighted that I tweeted almost immediately and then, just as quickly, came the derision "Fucking Larne? Why are you going to that hole? Why not come to Belfast, Derry?" and so on. Simple reason is, invitation. Invite me and I'll come. Other reason was talking to Martin Wilson at the Glasgow launch who thanked me for agreeing to come. That meant a lot to me. At the time of writing, Martin is the first nationalist mayor of Larne. That means a lot to me as well. Gary also picked me up at the airport and I have to admit, I was fucking loving this. You also get comments and snide remarks at events but these guys in the Station Bar were solid and I really enjoyed their company. And still do. So much so that I had a blistering show and loved every minute. It was from that comfort zone that someone asked me in the bar, whilst I was on stage "If this is all fucking true, why not sue them?" and then I tippled that it was a Hun. For all I love Larne, it's still Larne. Obviously I hadn't encountered this at any launch before and although I pride myself on quick wit, I reflected for a second and felt all eyes on me, it was one of those moments when you can hear the ice in the drinks melting so I looked at him and just said "I guess it's because they are dead and there is no one to sue" and held his stare by focusing on one eye (read that in a Steve McQueen book like) and the bar erupted in laughter much to my relief.

It was only lying in bed that night that I thought "It's Larne you stupid cunt, stop being so cheeky" but I guess I'm too old to change now. Or too stupid more like.

Most of my heroes don't appear on no stamp

It's at this point I should mention some of the heroes of this project. We've bonded enough now as writer and reader that I can introduce you to the family. Actually, let's leave the family till last. Of course I say some because I can't name all. One of the constant beacons of hope in this project was Graham Wilson. For all the slaggings and times on Twitter he seems to want to his throw iPad out the window, when the chips are down, he doesn't buckle. Which is handy because pretty much all the hate I received from so-called fellow Celtic supporters came almost immediately after he had interviewed me on air. Those shows killed. We always got an enormous reaction and the response was always breath-taking. Then, after a couple of hours, it would start. One person would start hissing insults at me, never directly, and try to get a reaction. They always did and it was almost always "What the fuck is your problem?" from good folk out there. I got one "supporter" once, a well-known self-entitled arsehole on Twitter who sees himself as an authority on everything. Only thing I can vouch for him being an authority on is his attempt at the most boring podcast of all time when he appeared on *Desert Island Tims* with Billy one night. He was one of three serial abusers who threw everything at me during this project. The other two, mid 60's bores, who took offense at The Asterisk Years because it didn't have any truck with their conspiracy theories, went out their way to be nasty to me. I always civil to them and, like I do with any abuser, tried to talk but it just went on and on and they are only not named because to do so gives them 1% of my piece of mind and they don't deserve even that.

The last Celtic fan, and I use that term very loosely, was the worst of all. He spent a long time spitting venom at Graham and then he started on me. Then he threatened my son. Then my Mother. I outed him at the end of August 2014 there. I know everything about him, his name, his address and even where he sits at Celtic Park. One day soon, he will be given the opportunity to repeat himself face to face with me.

I make no apology for that.

That's the stuff that hurts. I often discussed these incidents with Richard Swan and he would be aghast at what was going on. He talked me down from the ledge a few times, or clock tower I should say.

And by the way, if anyone thinks I'm playing the hard man here, read the fucking last part again. If you'd sit impassive at that you're not a better man than me, you're a stupid fucking cunt.

Jesus this is all getting a bit Franco Begbie here.

Haters gonna hate

Of course I knew the hate would come from Huns but the levels they went to staggered even me. Let me say again, I'm not the type who runs to the polis or a journalist when I get stuff like that. For days and weeks on end I was getting phone calls, threatening and sinister always. Twice the police came to my house, unannounced, and said I was in serious danger. Twice also I announced on Twitter I was going places and folk were waiting on me to have a quiet chat about the book. I pride myself on thinking on my feet and averted a bad situation both times with the bad feeling I had about them. Now I never say where I am going only where I have been.

One day at College I was sitting in an English class when the Learning Development Tutor came to the door and asked to speak to me. I followed him to an office and we made small talk but I was clueless as to what this was all about. We got to the office, I sat down and he closed the door behind us. He's not the most assertive guy at the best of times and I could see something was bothering him. He had 16 emails, from 16 different people (supposedly) all sent on the same day that all labelled me a bigot, a terrorist and various other bad things. He was baffled by it as I'd known him for a while and hadn't so much as whispered a code word to him. So I told him I thought it was in relation to a book I had just written and that I was well used to this kind of thing.

He went chalk white.

After I left, I sent Bob a message about what happened and he hit the roof. "It's fuckall to do with them!!!!!!!!!!!"

My education hung in the balance all weekend, it was a Friday I got pulled in, and all my teachers were asked for an opinion on me and this situation. Thankfully all stood up for me and I remained.

It was around this time as well that a few folk walked away from me. Some of them weren't really friends at all and had essentially tried to use me for their own end but one friend, real friend, just shut me out his life after one session in a pub. To this day I've no idea why because the three times I had contact with him since were when I didn't realise what was going on. If pushed, I reckon I know what happened. The day we were in the pub I was telling him about a lot of stuff that was going on. I'm going to make a leap here and say he went home, told his girlfriend, and they decided there and then to cut me out of their lives. In the meetings I'd had with her, I don't think she appreciated my "fuck the establishment" style. I might be totally wrong here but as they say in Brooklyn, what are you gonna do?

One particular incident happened though that meant I had to take action. I was walking home from college one day and a car sped up to me, tried to run me over, missed, u- turned and then threw a claw hammer at me with "Larkin Ya Fenian Bastard!!!" sound track. They missed and sped off.

This kind of thing has gone on over two years now. One incident still shocks me to this day. It was the Friday after the first Glasgow screenings of *The Asterisk Years* Documentary and I was heading up to my friend's house in Lochend for a couple of beers. I had decided to walk up and midway I was alerted to the fact that someone called Pete Lambie had absolutely slaughtered me and the film on Facebook. Not only that, but by the time I had got onto Facebook someone had posted my address as well. I have no idea if the two were connected by I took Lambie to task in a "What did I ever do to you?" type way. He tried to brush me off in an arrogant way but I wasn't having it. The stuff he had said about me was way out of line and I'm going stand up for myself. After this set to, I finally got to my mate Paul's house and tried to cool off. It was working right up until around 10pm when my phone vibrated a number I didn't know and it was a police officer. He asked me where I was and I got a bit paranoid so I asked him to confirm his I.D. and I then phoned Drylaw Police Station and they confirmed all I needed to know. What the police officer had told me was that one of the neighbours had called them after hearing a noise at my door. When said neighbour had investigated, he saw three men at my door and one of them had a sledgehammer and was trying to batter the door down. All three were mid to late 30s, baseball caps on and well built. When my neighbour opened his door the men got a fright and ran off.

So I had all this relayed to me over the phone as I made my home, not knowing what to expect. When I arrived the police had left after taking a statement from my neighbour and my door was off the hinges. I phoned the council emergency line and was told it would be Tuesday morning before they could fix it. This was Friday night remember. Effectively what I had to do was pretend the door was ok for the next four days until it was fixed.

All this had happened in the space of six-seven hours and my head was spinning. Especially when the next day I had arranged for my son James to meet the players. Well, even that was a story. The Legia Warsaw game was a nightmare for all but particularly my son James. The Legia hooligans had infiltrated where we were sitting and their behaviour left him scared. I had been on at Celtic previously saying they had made it too easy for Legia fans to get Celtic end tickets but concerns had fallen on deaf ears. After the game he was shaken up. He didn't want to go back to football games and I was raging. So I contacted Celtic and asked if they could do anything. The stress endured trying to get them to act was enough to drive the Dalai Lama bammy.

Months of calls, emails and texts and nothing was getting resolved. Eventually I got a sit down with Iain Jamieson, head of Celtic's PR department. I like Iain, as guy you couldn't meet anyone nicer, we are at odds with PR strategy (his obviously) but that's by the by. I sat down with him at Celtic Park and he agreed to do something for James. Except nothing happened. The frustration was bubbling to anger and that night, after the police phone and I stood on Leith Walk waiting on a bus in the pishing rain, I snapped and texted Iain. I would have phoned him but it was just past the 10.30pm cut off point and so I battered my phone and sent a message. It was an angry message. So angry that I think he was totally taken aback and replied "Who is this?" I told him who and he was pissed off, I could tell. So was I though and we then went onto have what is politely known as a "frank exchange of views". Believe it or not I don't get really angry that much but when it comes to my kids, if I perceive them being wronged, I have the tendency to be volcanic.

All this meant that after someone going for me online, then my address being posted and then my door being caved in, I was now taking my son in to meet the players the following day. Is that a window into how my life works? Almost. The following morning, door strategically placed to look locked, I picked James up and we took a bus to Princes St, making a slight detour to Wetherspoons in George Street for some breakfast. James took a seat and I went to the bar to order. I was about to put my card in the slot when a guy appeared behind the bar and said "Sorry, we can't serve you in here" I did a sort of half double take and said "What?" before he replied "it would be best if you leave" The barmaid looked as startled as I was. The guy then walked over to the till and cancelled my orders of two Scottish breakfasts as if he was ridding a bookshelf of *Mein Kampf*. He then came from behind the bar to "walk me out". I had two things in vision, my eldest son sitting at a table looking bemused the red mist that was descending in front of me. Rather than cause a scene, I whispered to the guy that I knew why he was doing this and just smiled at him using my best Norman Bates face.

It all sound horrendous this kind of stuff but it also inspires you.

And reminds you that this is Scotland.

Different Class

Why call a chapter different class? Well, let me pop holes in any potential theories right now (as if there would be any) and tell you the two reasons. Firstly, my auld man, who passed away in 1998, used to refer to anything good as "Different Class", so there's a little homage to him in there. The other thing is, as I've come to realise, the class system in the UK is what drives most things. As I've taken on people from the upper class, the elite if you will, I've came to realise they don't operate in any, way, shape or form as we do. Let me explain that further, they still do drugs, fuck, get pissed and cause bother, it's just that any consequence of that is swept away, brushed under the carpet or, quite simply, covered up. I've done a lot of bad things in my life. We were all on the rob as kids round our way, none of us had anything, so whether it was scrumping apples to stealing milk from the doorsteps of posh areas, we did it. We were almost always caught as well. The police caught me stealing football nets from Dunfermline College in Cramond one day when I was 13 and what happened to me? I was taken to the police station at Drylaw, this is back when it was still the old, Victorian, building, and battered by two cops. It scared the shit out of me but not as much as when they took me home, middle of summer and in full view of the entire street, and my auld man then battered me. I received another leathering in Drylaw police station when I was 17 after being huckled for fighting, area on area. This time I was bruised from below the neck right down to the toes. At no time did I ever think of complaining or going to a lawyer, you just accepted it and, in a lot of cases, wore it as a badge of honour. That was how it went with the police, you stepped out of line and they knocked fuck out of you in a dungeon.

So when I was told last year about the Edinburgh Establishment knocking fuck out of kids in dungeons, I paused for a while. See, the part of the story that didn't go in the book, was of a paedophile ring among the Edinburgh Establishment that centred round a flat opposite the Royal Commonwealth Pool in Edinburgh.

One day in the mid 90's, a prominent member of the Edinburgh Establishment walks into his luxury south Edinburgh home and announces that he has about a few months to live to his wife and family. They stand there aghast before asking the what, when, how and why questions. The man then spills it out "I'm HIV Positive". You see, for years, this man had been visiting a flat in Dalkeith Road in Edinburgh and regularly having unprotected sex with a succession of rent boys.

This flat was Edinburgh's version of the Elm Guest House.

It used to have a pineapple on the side of the building and this was how it was described to new visitors who needed directions. Many of the people mentioned in *The Asterisk Years* were regular visitors to this place. Now, when I was given this story, this was before the extent of establishment Paedophilia was known in the UK. Savile had been outed of course but many MP's hadn't and Kincora wasn't on the radar for most. I did as much digging as I could but hit a brick wall and, to my eternal shame, gave up, assuming that this kind of stuff would never be exposed. I dropped hints at book launches in 2013 about it and most got it but that was it. Then of course a lot of things broke in the media and the dominoes started to fall.

But not in Edinburgh.

The only paedophile that I know visited the flat and has been exposed is Sir Nicholas Fairbairn. Long since dead.

The rest though, remain free and unexposed. Just think about that. We know lots of people have been exposed after their death but not all got afforded that luxury. Not Rolf Harris, who painted a portrait of The Queen, not Max Clifford, who ensured that Establishment partied on and not Jonathan King.

But in Edinburgh, they remain unexposed.

Why?

This brings it backs to what I've said since the first time the words "Edinburgh Establishment" came out of my mouth. These people are untouchable. Way above the masons, out of reach of the media and living on a planet where they pick the judges, lawyers and police.

Remember, the press, the police and the judiciary are supposed to be completely separate. But *The Asterisk Years* Project told you that, in Edinburgh, this is not the case. The same postcode and streets are populated by all these people. Streets and postcodes that *The Asterisk Years* Project told you about, exposed and put in the mainstream. This was very similar to the hacking scandal at News International.

Everyone was in bed with everyone else. Often literally.

Yes these alliances were used by David Murray to prop up and propel a Rangers team that hadn't seriously challenged Celtic in decades. Yes they were able to cultivate alliances with Scotland's two prominent banks that meant unlimited credit lines and yes they were able to keep top Rangers players out of the clutches of the law but I say to you now that they have always ensured than an Edinburgh Establishment paedophile ring operated with impunity for decades.

Whilst it is our job to keep digging and hopefully expose these beasts, it also reminds us that they are a different class to us, and there's nothing good about it.

That's also why they were never caught and brought to justice.

Different Class.

Going Underground

You'll have worked out by now that a lot of this project was secret and there was more than one source. Bob is no more. One day he just disappeared. I couldn't get hold of him at all and realised soon that's how he wanted it. That happens, I tip my hat to him for being so honest, being a great host and setting me on this journey. I know he's still out there though. There were many other sources within this project and most of the work was done behind the scenes. Sometimes a source would just be a dialled-in Tim who was in the right place at the right time. Other times I get a tip and slipped someone a few quid and would have dynamite in my hands. My rule on that was if it didn't relate to the Murray era and could be stood up, then it went in my blog right away. These would cause quite a stir but none more so than the day I put up the letter that confirmed Sevco's status as a new club and that their first game, v Brechin, was played under the name Sevco. I should say now, I find it very hard to dig away for proof of Sevco being a new club. The fucking proof is they started in 2012, joined the Scottish League in the bottom tier and could not play in a UEFA competition for three years as per the rules on any new club. However, I know how it works in Scotland. We have PR men masquerading as journalists, pundits who thrive on an "Anyone But Celtic" agenda and a Rangers support who are the Scottish equivalent of The Tea Party. When Rangers died, some of those supporters started following Sevco. Fine, do what you want. Then though, backed by a compliant media and Spivs who would say anything to get those same fans cash, they started to perpetrate this myth that Sevco were indeed actually Rangers. Most people I know just laughed and shrugged their shoulders. Then though it was getting repeated and accepted as fact. Yes, these people were actually having you believe that Rangers somehow went into administration, were then liquidated but somehow magically escaped liquidation but were then relegated to the bottom league in Scotland.

On Twitter this became the focal point of a lot of people's lives and one day, knowing I had the information, I stupidly tweeted out that I would be releasing it soon. This led to the usual "Aye, sure" tweets from Huns but for some Celtic fans they would relentless in asking me when.

There was method in my madness.

Once Dundee Utd drew Sevco in the cup semi-final, you just knew that Operation:"Get Sevco To The Final" would swing into gear. So my thought was to drop the information on the Friday night before the game, 9pm to be exact, to try and underpin their confidence in any way I could. By this time, we were seeing all these daft hashtags from them about getting their "battle fever" on (whatever the fuck that is) and we knew they already had an enormous advantage in that they were playing the game at Ibrox, the stadium the new club had bought two years previous.

So I typed up the blog, loaded the letters on and clicked publish.

22,400 hits in one hour.

88,494 hits in one month.

354,656 and counting, total hits.

A lot of this type of information comes from sources so secret that you can't even joke about it. I would go on to publish several articles which would exposes the secrets and lies of Sevco as myself and one other person, kept digging and digging.

This other person would become the other main source in *The Asterisk Years* and be as important as anyone. As kindred spirits, we would bounce 100s of emails a day, a two pronged strategy of finding information for the documentary and exposing the lies that the PR men in the media would happily print in the name of Sevco and its employees.

I make no apologies for that.

Quite simply, I try and do anything I can to make Celtic supporters happy. That can mean plenty folk get upset, it can mean you put yourself in highly dangerous situations, it can mean greasing a few palms and it can mean going up a hell of a lot of dead ends.

Let me also say now, I'm no Woodward or Bernstein. I don't spend every waking minute at the computer or digging into people's lives but when I do, I know what I am doing. Let me qualify that. I trained as a journalist from August 1999 to June 2002. I worked at a local newspaper and gained journalistic qualifications. From there, I did a number of research jobs from 2003 to 2006. These ranged from digging up information on Johnny Adair to interviewing asylum seekers. (Hang on, that's kind of the same, you catch my drift though) I've also been writing for 15 years now. Now, as I've said before, I've never put myself up as a great writer but in the last few years I've become a pretty decent one, partly with the experience of books and partly because of the qualifications I now have. I also have an extensive range of contacts throughout the world. Most importantly though, I know how to listen. We don't live in a world of listeners any more. So I know when to shut the fuck up and that's a hugely important skill to have in this game. I talk to many people in the same game every day, from all sides of the spectrum, and that can be extremely helpful. Although there are some journalists who are utterly hopeless not all are and although they would recoil in horror if they were mentioned here right now (so I won't), they know who they are and, if you think about it, you should know who they are too. I've been led up the garden path by a couple of journalists. One was Stephen McGowan at the Daily Mail. I took him at face value but won't again. I'd had plenty contact with him in the past and told him at length why Dave King wouldn't be able to swoop in and save Sevco (this was at the time when King was releasing a statement on the hour, every hour). He was adamant he was and we batted stuff back and forth, totally good natured. Then, Ally McCoist was on one of his usual rants and told journalists that no player had received any bonus for winning division 3. I knew this was bollocks and rather than put it out there, I thought I'd send the info to Stephen to show I had no hard feelings. He took it and said he would take it to the editor right away.

I never heard from him again and the story never saw light of day.

Then of course there was the photo that ended up on the front page of the *Daily Record*.

David Murray had done everything he could to distance himself from Craig Whyte and I knew this was bollocks (The film showed that too) and so, in a way designed for maximum impact, I told everyone that I was releasing something big and one March morning, the photo went up on my website.

BOOM.

It exploded over the internet like a 16 year old with a free house and caused major ructions. My phone went bananas. Every major media wanted to buy it but I wasn't for selling. One had someone from their accounts department phone me and ask for bank details so they could transfer £7000 to me for the photo. I said no. It was upped to £12,000. I said no. I don't need to justify that to anyone. All I'll say is Justice for the 96.

Then in July, when the tickets for the premiere were going on sale, that picture appeared on the front of the Daily Record. Folk went nuts again. I should "sue the Record", they were "thieves", "how dare they" and so on.

This narrative continued most of the day until I got a DM from a close confidant which said "That was some coincidence that photo appearing on the front of the paper the day your tickets go on sale"

Aye.

By the way it was Keith Jackson who put the picture on the front page, Keith Jackson who had effectively been a PR man for Murray and various other clowns at Ibrox. He's one of the ones who did everything he could to protect Murray over the years and here he was ensuring a pic that nails Murray and Whyte on the same masthead, on the front page of Scotland's best-selling newspaper on the day the tickets for the premiere went on sale.

Cheers Keith.

The Tour

You'll always need a Yahmpy

There had been the premiere in Glasgow and a screening the day after that as well. Then there was a screening in Larne which was great as loads came from Belfast. Then there was one in Dublin which went so well, I could have ended it right there and then and then there was one in Irvine in the fantastic Celtic club down there. The final screening of the year was in Carluke, a day that will live long in the memory. Then though, I was taking it it to the world and the first stop was Philadelphia. On the first day, I made my way with Yahmpy to the Plough and Stars on Friday Jan 30th. The initial plan was to go the night before but President Obama was in town and that meant a lock down. In all these situations I am keen to test the film so when I spoke to the guy behind the scenes in the Plough on the Friday let's just say there was much merriment when he suggested I upload the film to YouTube so folk could just watch it from there. I say much merriment when of course I mean something else entirely. Things were sorted very quickly though and the rest of the evening was spent meeting old friends, making new ones and watching Yahmpy dodge hypothermia.

So to the day of the premiere and again I was keen to get in and ensure all was ok with the film. You'd be amazed at just how many people book the film months in advance and then test their equipment 15 minutes before it's due to be shown. No fears in Philly though as all promises were solid and it would be shown on two TV's so huge that you imagine the only other owner of the type is Tony Montana.

Graham Wilson appeared which was handy as he was MC for the day and we all made our way up to the An Gorta Mor memorial for a blessing from Father Brady. I said a little prayer for the film too. See I had no idea how it would be received and whilst everyone else is on a mission to drink as if prohibition was coming in on

Monday, I'm still standing like the naked art model seeing if anyone wants to paint me.

Thankfully, there was nothing to worry about. People showed fantastic respect to the film (Not easy in a rammed pub) and anyone who did fancy chatting was immediately told that they had had better ideas. The standing ovation the film received was a warm bath experience for me and the questions afterwards were insightful and fun to answer.

Philadelphia has a lot of solid Tims, most of whom have gone unrecognised for far too long but the likes of Seamus, Fitzy, Timothy, JohnJoe, Martin, Joe and the rest will live long in my memory.

After the success of the day, it was time for a chill out. I put myself in Graham's hands as we drunkenly wandered the streets of Philly looking for bars and restaurants. It sounds crap eh? It was absolutely brilliant as we just shot the shit and I could relax for a while.

Sunday morning, up with the lark, the zombies were slain.

By now I was exhausted and took the opportunity for some much needed kip post-match before taking in the Super Bowl that night.

Thoughts wandered to California as I was leaving for there in the morning despite dire warnings of storms and flight cancellations.
The bigger concern for me was I was taking my film to Sonoma County, a place I had never even heard of before I'd agreed to go, to be shown to be people I'd never met in my life before.

How's that going to work then?

Well I had plenty time to think about it. I woke at 4.33am in Philadelphia's historical district and was wide awake. Jet leg doesn't normally bother me much but it hung over me on this trip like an umbrella over the President when there is the chance of rain. It started on the Thursday. The previous day I'd taken a train down to Manchester to have a relaxing night before an early flight to Philadelphia. I'd got to the airport for 8am on one of those horrible mornings, when it's dark and cold and you'd rather stay in bed with Lorraine Kelly, but got checked in with minimum fuss which security then made up for by demanding I recreate *The Full Monty* before passing through. Manchester Airport Terminal 3 was being upgraded (to be fair, it needed it) so there was limited options to do anything other than sit in the terminal and hope that WiFi is part of that upgrade, preferably in the next five minutes. It was then it started to snow, the sort of snow that bothers even an Ice Road Trucker and it was clear this was going to be a problem. My flight was due to leave at 10.45am, the airport closed at 10.30am. As people clambered for information, flights all over the place started to be cancelled and I feared the worst. All the negative thoughts ran through my mind but the main one was what the fuck was I going to do if this plane wasn't getting off the ground today? I asked a Peter Kay lookalike/soundalike for an update and whilst he was genial enough, he clearly didn't have a clue what was happening. The Gods and the sun then shone on us and the snow ploughs were out clearing the runways, the main obstacle to us taking off and we were told we would be leaving at 1pm. I contacted Yahmpy, picking me up, putting me up and putting up with me for the next few days, he was cool about it(he's cool about most things) and I looked forward to getting on board, getting a film on and getting one of those meals that consist of mainly rice and tough meat.

I should have known.

The captain announced we would be leaving after the plane was de-iced and that it would take 20 minutes. Two films later and we were still sitting on the runway. It was now 4.30pm and frustrations were running high. People knew there was limited scope for us to now go on this flight, staff time and all that, and the worry was that we would be back off soon and back in deepest, darkest Manchester. This was commented on by a particularly cheery American guy who remarked breezily "Hey, do any of you guys think we will get off the ground?" Oh yes pal, there's a huge chance you will.

At 4.45pm we started moving. The feeling was like when you think the guy has just told folk the bar has closed and then your mate says "Don't worry, we are getting a lock in" and we were off. I don't normally sleep on planes but I even I succumbed thanks to this increasingly long day and Liam Neeson walking through the tombstones being about as entertaining as a night in with toothache.

The flight was non-eventful and I was boosted by the announcement that agents would be on the other side to help people re-book connections. This would give me a good run at bypassing most of the plane and getting to immigration first. For some people, this is a breeze, passport, fingerprints, photo, stamp, have a nice day but when you have a past as chequered as a flag at Formula One then you're always that wee bit keener to get it over with. I always scan for the person who looks the most affable and was mid this when I was called over by a guy who looked like he chewed wasps in his spare time. He gave me the third degree for what seemed like an eternity as he had an issue with the last time I was in America, New York in October, in that he refused to believe I was only there for a weekend. Like anyone in a uniform, it's pointless arguing with them, so I waited it out until he asked me what my job was and seemed happy about that (I actually said "Student" and I could tell he was thinking "Ah, I was right, he is an asshole") and the library like stamp was on the passport at last, he would lend America to me for the next three months should I need it that long.

Then came the wait at the baggage carousel, boredom alleviated when a sniffer dog took particular interest in a Keith Richards lookalike who remarked "Oh he probably smells my dog off me", Yeah ok, now touch your toes.

Finally out, I caught sight of Yahmpy who had the look of a guy who had a longer day than me. Understandable. He had taken the day off to pick me up at the airport at 1.45pm and the time now was a post-dinner chocolate mint. It had been our intention to go to The Plough and Stars to test the film but that intention was supposed to include things like daylight and slightly less exhausted bodies so we skipped home instead to South Jersey. I say skipped, Yahmpy drove and I sat in the comfiest seat I'd been in all day. President Obama was in town, umbrella and all, so Philly was on lockdown and I was glad to be in the warm confines of Yahmpy's new home and a wonderfully hospitable welcome from his wife Christine. I've been in situations in the past where I have been made to feel unwelcome in someone's home and it's a horrible feeling. Similarly, since a lot of bad shit has happened to me in the last 18 months, I make it a rule to never stay with strangers and with Yahmpy being pretty far from that and Christine putting me at ease immediately, I was delighted to be with them.

Yahmpy's fridge had a selection of beers to suit a beer experimentalist but that's not me so it wasn't long before I was in a cosy guest room for the six hours sleep I'd get before the inevitable jet lag kicked in. Jet lag has a weird way of making you feel totally fresh after a sleep, it's just that it's about five hours before everyone else wakes up.

So Friday was a long God damn day made better by visits to the Philly diner and of course, the Plough and Stars for the Feile.

California Love

But that's for another day. Right then I was leaving Philly the morning after the Sevco slaying wasn't going to be straight forward. The north east of America was being battered by snow storms and the departures screen at the airport glared at me with cancellation written so much it was like it had been given lines as a punishment. My flight was still going though but the numbers in the departure lounge worried me. There were only about 12 people sitting there for a flight due to leave in 40 minutes. Investigating like Columbo, the flight was still going and the pilots had even arrived. We awaited our plane to arrive from Raleigh (North Carolina not Walter) and ended up boarding 30 minutes late. This was a worry, I was only flying to New York and had just a 58 minute layover, then I saw the reason there were so few people there, the plane was an 18 seater. The scheduled flight time was 40 minutes but the pilot said we would be in the air for 15 which started to assure the worried faces who were all thinking "storm, tiny plane, storm, tiny plane" and there was pretty much chop the whole time but 20 minutes later I was queuing for my next plane to San Francisco from JFK and was feeling pretty good. We were boarding early and this plane was huge, all was good. Right up until I sat down, looked out the window and saw a snow storm that would have put off Captain Scott. Needless to say the runway was closed and we were delayed two hours, before my second plane de-icing of the trip. I didn't relax until we were in the air.

Touching down in SFO, late but happy, my cousin Tony was there to pick me up and whisk me away to his house. I had a couple of days there before heading to Sonoma County and was able to meet Tony's kids for the first time. No jokes, it was magical. Wednesday we drove up to Santa Rosa, which took about 90 minutes, and checked into the Hotel La Rose with minimum fuss. What was very noticeable all around the streets was *Peanuts*. And Charlie Brown, plus Snoopy too. Turns out Charles M Schulz ended his days in Santa Rosa. We decanted to a local bar as happy hour was just starting and alerted Peter Meechan, my contact for this screening, who got back immediately and said he would be there in 20 minutes, always a good sign. I'd been in town a few hours and it occurred to me that I was as far from home as I've ever been and here I am showing a film here. Who the hell is going to be interested in this? This far out you expect a Peter type guy to be all about the hoops and maybe one or two more but that's it. Anyway, Peter duly arrived and had two other guys with him (Good, at least there would be five of us at the screening) and we all immediately hit it off. I'd wrongly assumed Peter was an ex-pat but he was more American than Apple Pie and his two buddies, Jimmy and Isaac were exactly the same. As usual though, that combination of Celtic and good alcohol enabled bonds to be made and before long we were all laughing, joking and talking all things Celtic. This was magic. Here I am in wine country, California and I'm talking Celtic with three great guys. Bliss. We hit a few more bars and drank until closing time before the guys walked us back to our hotel. There was no need to do that but that's just the kind of guys they are.

Next morning, slightly delicate and a head cold developing, we were picked up at 12 (there had been talk of a 7am pick-up the night before through beer bravado, this was never happening) and whisked off for a day of wine tasting. I've tasted plenty wine but I've never been wine tasting and obviously my main point of reference was the movie *Sideways*. We did a few different places with the highlights being Limerick Lane, which tied me in particular up for a while, and Francis Ford Coppola's place which not only had great wine, a swimming pool and a stunning setting but also had lots of different things pertaining to his movies (the gold telephone from Godfather

2, Dracula's suit, Robert Duvall's surf board from Apocalypse Now) and all the Oscars he has won. You may not be that impressed, my jaw was on the fucking floor the whole time.

Friday was the screening and that meant rest up before it. My head cold was awful and I needed a sleep. Isaac came to pick us up at 6 so we could go to Jasper O'Farrell's in Sebastopol and set the movie up. We had a few issues but got there in the end and that's when I took stock and realised the bar was packed. There were seven guys up from San Francisco but everyone else was local. This blew me away but not as much as the kind welcome I was given by almost everyone (one lunatic woman managed to annoy everyone in the bar) and blistering night took place with Jimmy as MC making Jay Leno look like an amateur and the film going down a storm. A lovely kicker was the bar had its best ever night. So much so that they were happy to give me 15% of the takings. I reacted with one of my many double takes of this trip. Those takings got split between Mary's Meals and The Kano Foundation and a perfect night was complete with new friends made and lifelong bonds created.

We got about two hours sleep before up for the Dundee game (430am ko) and let's just say things weren't quite as boisterous now. The San Francisco Bhoys joined us and were great craic again. The host, Lucas, even did a great breakfast but it was tinged with sadness because when it was done so was I and I knew I would be saying goodbye.

Schulz ended his days in this part of the world, my theory is he visited, met Peter, Jimmy and Isaac and just stayed forever.

My last day in California meant a day in San Francisco. I'd been once before but that was 1987 and so I was looking forward to it a lot. Being driven from Santa Rosa was perfect, took about 45 minutes and among beautiful scenery. It gave me the chance to reflect as well, the previous night had saw a packed bar watching *The Asterisk Years* in a place I hadn't even heard of six months ago. One of the questions I get asked is why certain people, in the media or on the lunatic fringes of it, never mention the film. I used to give a few different opinions on this but Santa Rosa made me realise: Who gives a shit? Most, if not all, of these people are in the game for a career or to protect one and therefore their opinion matters to me as much as Bomber Brown's. What I care about is what the people in the street think. I'd shut myself down for good before I'd go down the road of doing or saying anything controversial just to stay relevant. Which of course we all know they would be doing if the film was shite, so their only weapon is ignorance from an ivory tower. How ironic.

San Francisco is a beautiful city and I loved being there but I was itching to get back to New York. Anyone who knows me knows how big a bearing the city has had on my life. I was on the red eye from SFO and incredibly we boarded on time with no weather issues on this balmy Californian night. All was good as we got ready to taxi to the runway when...BANG! A coffee pot explodes. So we have to wait twenty minutes on a guy to come and rip it the fuck out, something I could have done in two seconds, before leaving. Incredibly, some middle aged woman piped up "Wait, does this mean there's no coffee on the flight now? Can't we wait til we get a new coffee pot?" A few of us looked at each other in that "Yeah, I'm in if you want to throw her out the window" kinda way but thankfully the stewardesses were in no mood to indulge this cry baby. What it did mean though was there were no films or TV on the plane which suited me as I had three seats on the plane to myself and could stretch out. I could never normally sleep on planes but have slept on all bar the short one on this trip. Thank you God. Hitting JFK at 5.30am, I was in my hotel in Manhattan for 6am, finally finding the half hour the traffic isn't crazy in New York.

It was great to be back.

New York's Green and White

I was back in October and so normality had crept in again, something that hadn't taken place for me in New York for almost a decade and when my head hit the pillow, it felt good being alive. Or as good as it can be at 6am on a Sunday morning.

My friends from Nairn, James and Donna, were flying into Newark at 12pm and we were meeting up with Jock Kennedy and Frankie Fraser at Grand Central at 2pm to be picked up by Chas Duffy to go to a screening in The Bronx. They arrived incident free and it was great to see everyone again, in particular Chas and Kev Devine whom I didn't know would be there. There was that lovely "never been away" feeling as we sped up the FDR and poked fun at MetBhoy Frankie as we passed Yankee Stadium.

I lived in The Bronx for two years and most of it was an unhappy experience but that Sunday Chas, Kev and everyone who packed out *Ireland's Thirty Two* washed that all away with the skill of an Upper West Side window cleaner. It was made even better as Yahmpy and family made another appearance too. It was a great day and great catch up and another box ticked in the promises I'd made around this film.

James, Donna and I had intended to get the Metro North from Woodlawn back into the city but decided instead to call in on the most bizarrely named cab firm in the world (*Break To The Border*) and just taxi it back to midtown. We hit *Faces and Names* on West 54th St but the guys were struggling and went to bed for around 10pm. I was buzzing though and knew my best friend on the planet would be in midtown for 11. It's hard to overestimate what Gary and I have been through but needless to say it was like we had never been away. He came bedecked in Celtic colours and just added another reminder that New York is indeed green and white. We talked and drank the night away in *O'Lunney's* and things seemed normal again.

I've struggled with a lot of past shit affecting my mental state but I've moved on and feel stronger, better.

Monday came and I took the Nairn crew to the village and Little Italy. My *Donnie Brasco* obsession meant another visit to the *Mulberry Street Bar* (formerly *Tony's Bar*) before my *Sopranos* obsession meant another visit to *Cha Cha's* restaurant for sausage and peppers.

We went back to the hotel via Union Square and a look at America's debt before decanting to *Jimmy's Corner* for some cheap beers before a meal that could choke a buffalo in *Virgil's*. Of course, I shouldn't have been doing any of this, I should have been in Boston but an almighty snowstorm put paid to that. I was gutted because I love Boston but not a single mode of transport was available.

Tuesday I knew would be a day off so I had already made my mind up to take the guys to Queens and see some of New York that the tourist guides won't tell you about. So we did a good diner on Queens Boulevard and had a little walking tour before going to *Donovan's* in Woodside for an afternoon drinking. Except it was closed. Frustrated, we took the 7 train back to Manhattan not realising fate had just played her hand. Through a serious of bizarre circumstances, far too strange even to relay here, two hours later we were sitting in the *Ed Sullivan Theater*, the one The Beatles changed America in, watching a live recording of the David Letterman show. It's hard to describe how surreal this was. I'm an avid fan of Letterman and at times it felt like I was watching the best HD picture ever.

Minds blown, we decided to have a big night out in Hell's Kitchen and I'd like to say I was the target of a cougar except a friend in Cali pointed out that I am too old to regard anyone as a cougar.

A drunken night was had by all though and Gary put in another appearance.

Wednesday was game day, for Celtic at Firhill and me at *Jack Demsey's*. So I watched Celtic at Firhill in *Jack Demsey's*. This gave me a chance to hook up with Big Tommy again, the lynch pin of the NY Fenian Bhoys. Guys like Tommy are one in a million. In fact, ten million. Another successful screening ensued and this part of tour was over.

Jack Demsey's gave me a chance to meet a whole load of new Tims and reaffirm my belief that the fans are the club. These are the people I made this film for, not for the press, the careerists or the critics, but the folk for whom Celtic is a way of life. I was given gifts by most of them and that's the best aspect, a recognition that we are in this together. Celtic have millions of these people all over the world and through the film I've met over 2000 of them since November. They are the ones who suffered most through the two decades of cheating, which explains why they get it and probably answers why others don't.

Oh, and God Bless America.

Next stop Australia. Kindae.

Defiance

In between times there whee trips all round Scotland and one to London too.

I documented Coatbridge and Airdrie in *Anyone but Celtic* with the nod to Winchburgh too.

There had been a trip to Drogheda, a night excellently organised by Harper, Joe and the St Laurence's CSC. It was a great and eventful night with me travelling up with Conor and Mick, expertly driven by Dublin Dessie. I had a great time with a few of their members whilst big Conor managed to collapse midway through the event, claiming to be tripped up, whist folk, Harper in particular, were boogieing on down on the dance floor.

There was a great weekend of gigs in Alloa and Cumbernauld in venues that, to the uninitiated, you might think are a bit rough but always end up being filled by the best people. In Alloa, Martyn Cassidy ran a great night. I'd never even been to Alloa before but getting lifted and laid always helps. The next night was the Mallard in Cumbernauld and I was blown away to be given a special *Asterisk Years* decanter by the great Liam Sinclair.

All the while the message was growing and so to was the amount going to charity. This was exemplified by The Den Social Club.

After a great screening, where I even got an Asterisk Years cake from the lovely Dawn Gray, there was over £3000 raised for The Kano Foundation. At the time of writing, The *Asterisk Years* has helped raise £20,000 for various charities and yet always in the backdrop of snipers.

You see a couple of people took exception to me raising money for the Kano Foundation. One did it from behind a mic and another did it behind my back. They went after the Kano, they went after me and anyone who dared stand up to them got it in the neck. We knew right away who was behind it and the amount of folk who stepped up ready to hit back was incredible. It would have been so easy to do so but definitely the wrong move. Huns or "Tims" folk like that want to derail you, bring you down to their level and the best response is to hold your head up higher, stick your chest out further and keep going.

I learned that in Coatbridge and Airdrie. I learned that in London too from the Wimbledon CSC. All young guys who are flying the flag high down there and who were an enormous inspiration to me, not least because they ran a great night that always had an episode I'll never forget. After the film, I did my usual Q&A and was leaving the high stage when a really big bloke came purposely towards me. I scanned the room and everyone seemed to be pre-occupied and I'm thinking "Aw naw, this is it" as he got nearer I realised he was easily 6 foot 3, 240 pounds and fearsome. He grabbed me, pulled me close and screamed in my ear "I'm Chelsea, I'm Celtic and I've battered hundreds of fascist's dan here mate!!!!!"

How can you fail with people like that on your side?

Down, down, deeper and down

I left my house in Edinburgh at 3pm and got three buses to Glasgow Airport. All went smoothly until, having just passed through security, the plain-clothes plod wanted a word. The main guy was very interested in me.

He particularly wanted to know what I did for a living and could I then explain what my last book was? I thought there was no point in beating around the bush (there or here) and said "It was about Rangers cheating" and he said "And you earn money from that?" with a look that suggested I had just asked him if he wouldn't mind phoning his wife and asking her if she fancied joining the mile high club. He seemed satisfied though and walked away upon which his co-colleague said "I loved the book" with a big smile on his face.

Good cop/Bad cop.

The flight was delayed an hour due to high winds but no real problems on a 7 hour flight as the time was made up pretty easily. I flew Emirates and Economy class was as good as I've ever been on. After an incident free journey, I was in Dubai and 80 degree heat with the airport having no real grasp of air conditioning. It was only a two hour layover though and before long I was on the best plane I've ever seen. This was a floating palace. A sneak peek at first class showed me a country club type set up that the likes of Harper are at home with.

13 hours, eight Sopranos episodes, four red wines and two great meals later I was in Melbourne.

I always worry going through any immigration check, a mixture of working class guilt and paranoia with a dash of realism but it's made easier when the border security guy says "How you going, mate?" A few basic questions later (Asking where I was staying and giving the impression he would put me up if I was stuck) and I was on my way to meet Sean Fitzgerald (Pictured, first right) I've known Sean for about 15 years and within 15 seconds the craic was flowing. It was 6.30am and pitch black but the sun rose as we drove through Melbourne and even that brief glimpse from the car made me realise it was beautiful.

Crashing at Sean's place (That's me not the car), the fight was on to fight the jet lag and given it was only 7.30am that was going to be about as easy as writing this in complete darkness currently is.

Sean had a few things to do and I succumbed to a kip for about an hour. Sean, and later his wife Maeve (Pictured, first left) made me feel so welcome. That is the key to any of these trips and really relieve any stress.

At night we went out dinner, a Greek place called Risk, with Sean and Maeve's friends Michael and Margaret (Pictured, centre, you can tell who is who ffs) and had a brilliant laugh as Michael is originally from Edinburgh and so we shared tales of the oul' country.

After this, it was back to Chez Fitzgerald and a few beers before I had to fall into my bed before I fell on the floor somewhere (lack of sleep not too much drink) and got a decent kip until 5am (Handy given what time the game is on Saturday morning) but would still have liked to knock out the jet lag in one go given the mammoth journey.

If you made it this far, I hear you and thank you, I know exactly you feel.

Melbourne Rebels

And so to The Australian Premiere of The Asterisk Years, to be held in The Pint on Punt in Melbourne. Sean and I had gone down on the Friday to ensure everything was running smoothly and, in no short part thanks to Pat Close, things were eventually. Bottom line with this tour is the film is the be all and end all and when folk ask me if I ever get nervous, my reply is always the same in that I am nervous until I know the equipment is working fine, everything falls into place after that.

Saturday was day of the premiere and, as luck would have it, a head cold visited me and was about as welcome as an immigrant in UKIP. That being said, a nice relaxing build up was ensured when a friend from back home, Aaron, appeared and helped drown out the band that was on before us and almost made me want to belt out a few myself.

The guys at the Jock Stein Melbourne CSC, Sean, Pat and Colin in particular, did a fantastic audition for *Changing Rooms* and transformed the pub into a cinema in no time.

The place filled up nicely as folk appeared from all around, some even came in a stretch limo, one guy flew in from Tasmania and I think the entire Hughes family was there. Before long the bar was packed and we were on.

The film got a fantastic reception and I was bowled over by the love and respect I was shown by the people there. You're always going to be a little apprehensive how it will go down, especially down under this far from home but then you realise you are home. If the world has done anything to me in the last year then it has shrunk. The Bhoys and Ghirls in Melbourne and surrounding areas are flying the flag high and wide and the strength of feeling here is as strong as it is in the Gallowgate.

After a quick break, it was time for the Q&A, expertly set up by Pat and expertly run by Sean, as lots of good questions came in. Most people will know I will answer anything. Quite a few folk would ask a non-serious question (I think!) before a serious one and were probably shocked when I was happy to answer both. Which meant hilarity among the crowd ensued a few times.

None more so than from the last question.

You get a sense when there will be a "But" coming in a question and this one was set up just like that. A deep breath and then "Why don't you support Hibs?" There was just a hint of accusation in it and the implication with it that coming from Edinburgh, that's who I should support. Now, far be it from me to make judgements, but I didn't think it was the most sensible question to ask given we were 12,000 miles from Paradise and in a room full of more countries than Google Maps and more creeds than the Rocky movies. As I answered as best and politely as I could "Are you f*****g radge ya c**t?" (Kidding) one of the Bhoys immediately kicked in and said to the guy "I'm from Belfast, who should I support?"

It was all good though and I spent the rest of the evening having a brilliant craic with all the Bhoys and Ghirls there before pitching my tent beside some new friends Jill and Loretta who were great company albeit terrible dancers.

Before long, a proper singer was on, and the songs of Rebellion were in full flow.

There was also a raffle which raised $850 for the Sacred Heart Mission of St Kilda.

I was surprised by the gift of a specially commissioned shirt (Pictured) marking the occasion but on reflection I shouldn't have been. It was simply another example of the welcome in Melbourne.

Thank you all, Rebels.

Next stop Brisbane.

Spiders Paradise

With a heavy bag, and even heavier heart, I left the capable hands of Sean and Maeve in Melbourne and flew up to The Gold Coast. I arrived a little early at Melbourne airport and I do mean a little. I was there one minute before I could check in and was sent to the back of the queue. This allowed me to go and buy a pair of sunglasses (Note to reader: if you ever go to Australia, NEVER go without sunglasses). It has to be said that for all Melbourne is great, boy is it expensive. I know it's an airport bar and all that but fish and chips with a pint for $39 marketed as a "deal" then you know your plastic will be burnt.

I flew JetStar and was told to expect "Australia's Ryanair" but this was miles ahead. No fuss, no standing queueing for days on end and we were up and away before you could sell a scratch card.

Touching down in The Gold Coast I had really little idea of what to expect. One thing I certainly didn't expect was Chris McMonagle waiting on me as soon as I got off the plane. Normally you get off, get the bag and go meet whoever your meeting but not for the first time I was told "Remember, this is Australia"

The other thing I didn't expect was to be picked up in an Aston Martin. Chris and I would probably have Roger Moore spitting the dummy more than he did about Idris Elba.

The picture with this blog is the main part of The Gold Coast aka Surfers Paradise and this is what faced me as we sped off in the car.

(Pause for reflection: I've been driven to pubs where ambulances have their own parking spaces and the tables and chairs look like they have been borrowed from Slade Prison, now I'm being driven through Surfers Paradise in an Aston Martin. Thanks Chris, Brisbane, Australia, all of you, God, Allah and everyone else who knows me)

We arrived at Chez McMonagle, very similar to the Montana house in *Scarface,* and I settled in. Chris has a wonderful wife, Susan, who made me feel welcome immediately. I can't over emphasise how much that means to me.

The next few days were spent on the beach, in bars and restaurants and listening to Chris' stories (good and bad-That's for you Martin) and meeting new people.

Wednesday night was memorable, sitting on a deck outside Chris' house, sharing stories with Eddie, Stuart and Martin, drinking cold Heineken and eating a fantastic curry. There have been a few low points in this project, some real dark moments but these are the times that even the score on that score.

Thursday I went around with Chris as he did a few jobs and anyone who knows him will know how interesting that can be before hitting the worst Greek restaurant in Australia and then a night on the bevvy in Surfers Paradise.

If this all sounds like a doss then I can tell you why, it is. Every so often you meet guys like Chris who just can't do enough for you and it's easy to get swept up in it.

Our street cred did fall a fair bit though as we were in one bar, The Boat House, and we had a visit from the law. When a guy in a police uniform comes towards you and he's armed more than Rambo then you do clench just a little. When it's a guy who has already given you a bottle of Vodka as a welcome gift and whose brother and father have played for Celtic, you then relax a little.

Friday and it was off to Brisbane.

As you get with a lot of places, a little bit of internal politics meant some from the area weren't going to attend. Something that happens a lot but never ceases to amaze. It was no problem though as plenty came from miles around and a fantastic night was had by all. Chris went above and beyond again and the craic was brilliant all night, especially with Sean, Martin, Eddie, Pat, Johnny and Jim.

Martin and his band Black Stove played and yours truly ended up singing The Wild Rover and Sean Sabhat with them.

It was that sort of night.

Lots of love and respect came my way and I thank everyone for my time in Queensland, none more so than Chris.

With that being said, in his infinite wisdom, Chris thought it would be ok to drop off everyone in 200 mile radius after the screening meaning your intrepid writer currently has eyes on stilts.

I can't complain though, in the midst of the journey a huge spider got into the car which forced Chris' son Kieran to pull over and as we awaited its attack on me. I somehow managed to usher it out the car and had no time to panic as I felt Chris' hand on my shoulder and him laughing with "There's your blog right there!!!!!"

Cheers, Sydney

I flew down from The Gold Coast on Saturday afternoon to Sydney. Another minimum fuss flight that was improved massively by Stephen Harvey with a Qantas Executive Club invitation. In reality that was free bevvy and finger food and so my thirst suddenly came on as I entered.

I was met on arrival at Sydney Airport by Jim Reilly and Jim Kinlan of the Sydney City CSC.

Jim Kinlan has been the rock that this tour down under was built on and it was good to be met by friendly faces and whisked away to a hotel quicker than I moved back and forth to the bar in that Executive Club for the chilled Peroni on tap.

The screening was almost immediately after touchdown and the venue was Cheers in Sydney, expertly organised by the lovely Vanessa McGuire. It was a good sized crowd there and the film down well with almost everyone (more of that later)

The MC was Albert, who did a fantastic job at the Q&A and all books were sold faster than the steepest train in the world travels in the Blue Mountains.

It was a raucous Saturday night crowd but the vibe was good and I met some fantastic people like Steff, Sydney's best barber, and Brian, the loudest man in Sydney,

I was also honoured and privileged to have a drink bought for me, for the first time ever, by the one and only Brian McAvoy. Unfortunately there was no sign of Skippy the 6-2 Kangaroo or indeed another round from Brian.

After the show, it was game time, ICT v Celtic, and the least said about that the better.

Jim Kinlan was looking after me and after saying cheerio to all, we were in a taxi and back to the digs.

I had a warm glow after that night, given the fantastic welcome and great people I met.

This made it all the more bizarre when someone at the screening started attacking me and the film online all through the night. The crux was that it was all lies and that I was down in Sydney to make money from it. Everyone is entitled to their opinion but if you've been in my company all night and said nothing, then do a sneak attack online, you're entitled to f*** all. (For the record, I paid my own way)

Incidentally, this was no reflection on the Sydney City CSC.

They reinforced how good a friend they have been to me with a wonderful day on Sunday spent at "The Rocks" with Jim Kinlan, Jim Reilly, Kieran Fanning, Paul Lygate and Ron Dorran, the latter two especially keeping me captivated all day.

Brian McAvoy even put in an appearance but reverted back to type and no drink was forthcoming this time.

It was back to the hotel then and this time a different room (Anyone who has heard Jim Kinlan snore will know why)

I did all the tourist things and took a boat to Manly Bay on Monday. We went to the Hotel Stayne for a quick refreshment and were met by the manager Michael who happily informed us "Fenians drink for free"

After that it was off to Penrith for a couple of days with Jim, his lovely wife Linda and son Josh.

Again, an incredible welcome and hospitality throughout.

The last day bookended the trip by spending the day around Bondi Beach with the two Jim's and generally having fun before being driven to the airport for the five hour flight to Perth.

Sydney was wonderful to me. Despite the obvious drawback, it didn't in any way altar my feelings towards it or the wonderful people I met there.

The flame will never die there.

As for abuse? That's all good too now but then again, maybe that is down to my bodyguard in Australia (Pictured)

Thanks Lomalito.

Perth Glory

Leaving Sydney, I had a great day at Bondi Beach with Jim Reilly and Jim Kinlan. They dropped me off at the airport and I was sitting reading my Kindle (The Sex Lives of Siamese Twins, actually) when I saw a guy in a suit careering towards me in a similar fashion as a park keeper would when you're playing football in front of a 'No Ball Games' sign. I pretended to continue to read before the inevitable "Excuse me Sir, Can you follow me please?" when he said "I'VE JUST BEEN READING YOUR BOOK!!!" and I just managed to side step heart failure. I'm way beyond saying "What one?" now so Phillip, if you're reading, hope you enjoyed pal.

Arriving in Perth five hours later, I was met by Paddy McOnie and Andy Gordon from the Perth, WA CSC. This is always the key moment in these things, will you get on, will they like me, will we have a rapport but, within five minutes of standing at the baggage carousel, I knew I was in safe hands. By the time we were in Paddy's pick up, we were all laughing and joking and that was a good sign. Arriving the hotel, I checked in and was met by the most cantankerous receptionist since Basil Fawlty.

Next day I explored a wee bit of Perth before meeting up again with Andy as well as Davy, Brian, Chris and a couple others of the Perth Bhoys. If The Asterisk Years film has a heaven, it's in Rosie O'Grady's, Perth. Talk about a perfect venue, I was shown around it and it had every single thing you hope for at any venue which meant two days of relaxing for me (Some will say that's all I do, I know, particularly Liam "Delegate" Power)

On Friday, it was off to Manduah with Andy and Raymie (who drove), Raymie is one of those forces of nature you meet every so often and this meant non-stop craic on the hour drive down, snaking through the beauty that is Western Australia and we arrived in Mandurah, another idyllic setting, to meet Kev O'Neill and the Mandurah CSC who presented me with a hat, badge, and shirt from the CSC that I was choking to wear as soon as I saw. It was amazing to be in such a remote location and see a big Celtic beating heart and that is credit to Kev and the Bhoys.

Next day was the day of the screening and I had a few hours to kill so Davy drove me to Fremantle so I could go to the prison and see the sight of the first great escape.

There was a brilliant atmosphere in Rosie O'Grady's that night due in no small part to the fantastic organisation of the club. You won't find a bigger, better or more organised CSC on the planet despite it being 12,000 miles from Paradise.

The screening was fantastic and the Q&A a hoot. I loved it.

Sunday, a little delicate, was game day and, unlike Meekings, I can't handle that one.

Thankfully we had the Catalpa MFB at half time to entertain us and my God did they do that.

Monday and it was time to go home. Every so often I get days that I hope will never end. I was rough as sandpaper when I met Andy to go to Fenians Pub then Rosies and by 2pm I couldn't look at a drink. Paddy McOnie, as usual, had the answer, "Good Guinness" and went back in Paddy's pick up to another Irish bar where we drank, laughed and talked all day before Paddy's son, Chris, took me to the airport after I had said my goodbyes.

Perth washed away every germ of the entire Asterisk Years project due to the love and respect I got there, not to mention laughing non-stop for five days.

I was sad to leave Australia but proud to know that Celtic are being represented by Tims who don't bend and don't compromise for anyone.

My Asterisk Paradise

This is the end as Jim Morrison once said. Not that he started all this. In fact, in this trilogy of *By Any Means Necessary: Journey with Celtic Bampots*, *The Asterisk Years: The Edinburgh Establishment versus Celtic* and *Anyone but Celtic*, there were two people who inspired it more than any. The first I'll leave you to read about in the next book. The other was Malcolm X (Which I am sure some of you worked out anyway).

Today *The Asterisk Years* hits Celtic Park for what is the last ever public showing in Scotland. This blog will be the last time I ever write about a screening as well. After a tour that would drain energy from the national grid, it's time to a draw a line under a project that has seen me have more thrills and chills that Stephen King, more ups and downs than the lift in the Empire State Building and meet more new people than the guy who has a position vacant in this Tory hell we live in. We have come a long way in this project and travelled even further spreading the word.

It's been a blast.

Whilst there have been threats and abuse throughout, the support I've received personally and the film has received in general has been overwhelming, inspiring and humbling. It helped me overcome the long, lonely dark nights, the snipers, the thugs, the people with two faces and the apathetic.

This was a film made for a budget less than a Sevco war chest and faced more hurdles than Liu Xiang but, somehow, we got to the end and were well received everywhere we went and by almost everyone who saw it.

It has become both the platform and the standard for future projects.

Critically though, it was funded, supported, promoted and defended by the people in the streets and that's what matters to me most. Forget the written press, TV, cable channels or guest spots on *Off The Ball*, it is the people in the streets who matter most because they are the ones who suffered the most through two decades of cheating.

For now though, it's time to look forward not back. Tonight, we are on our way to Paradise and soon we are coming back with a new book, audio book and film in 2015 and 2016.

The key point in all this that this project came as a result of citizen journalism. That's when a radge Gadgie like me does something and then comes to radge Gadgies like you and says "Come and join in my chorus" Daunting? Yes. Exciting? Very.

So I guess what I am saying is, thank you. Thank you for sticking by me, even in the darkest times, and believing in this project. It had to be done by people like us because we never expect nor want help from anyone else.

I'll leave you with a quote that I think is apt:

"I just don't believe that when people are being unjustly oppressed that they should let someone else set rules for them by which they can come out from under that oppression"

Malcolm X

More than a convention

What happens in Vegas, stays in Vegas. Until Brian McAvoy goes and photographs everything from the beer he's drinking to the security people escorting him to his bed. The 2015 NAFCSC Convention was my fourth time attending and easily the best.

It was a new hotel, The Westgate, after the setback of The Riviera going into liquidation in May (insert your own Rangers joke here) and the intervention of Michael Luther who broke the news to Tam Donnelly and assured him he would find him an alternative.

And what an alternative.

Elvis Presley played, and sold out, The Westgate for eight solid years and it was easy to see why. As much as I loved the character of The Riv, The Westgate was a cut above it. At $4 a beer as well, with Tims everywhere and gorgeous sunny days aplenty then this may well be heaven.

The Pool Party kicked things off on the Tuesday with a never-to-be-forgotten rendition of "Do The No Promotion" belting out for most of the day. My skin burns when someone flicks a lighter on so I watched on from the shade as Tims from everywhere, of all shapes and sizes, had the time of their lives.

Wednesday was my big day, with *The Asterisk Years* showing. I'd got to Vegas on the Sunday and, like he always does, Tam had everything sorted out for me already. It's hard to overegg how great a guy Tam Donnelly is but he was made to run things like this and I watched him go from having to deal with massive, hundreds of thousands of dollars problems to ensuring a couple were having a good time in a matter of seconds. Tam is a leader but he also cares and applies the type of organisation that was matched only by Jacky Meehan before he retired. I say "retired" but Jacky is always there to help and, like Tam, has the street-fighter smarts surrounded by a heart of gold.

4pm on the Wednesday was the film showing and over 100 people showed up. I was blown away by that. It's Vegas and everyone is there to party (get pished) so I was humbled by the turnout.

I was then blown away by the kind, and totally unexpected, words from Tam post film, on stage, and I don't mind admitting to you that plenty tears were wiped away.

Wednesday night was cabaret night with Hugo Strainey and Pat Rolink, two guys that were born to entertain.

I spent a lot of the week helping out in The Fed office as it was ran expertly by Mike Boyd from Chicago. Mike has been a good friend of mine for a long time and if Tam and Jacky are the street-fighters, Mike is Tom Hagan. His ability to put a cool head in amongst any problem is a vital component in a week like this.

Apart from helping Mike, being in The Fed office allowed me plenty time in the company of Tony Donnelly (Tam's brother) and Pat (no second name as it could affect his giro) and listen to some of the best stories and patter you'll ever hear.

Arriving on the Wednesday night were John Paul and Kerry from Celtic, armed with the task of promoting the club and its services and a fine job they did too.

The Green Night was Thursday and a chance for The Paddy Ryan Band to get going. Charlie and The Bhoys were curtailed by Visa problems so Derek Warfield and The Young Wolfe Tones kicked off what ended up being a raucous, riotous night to remember with Paddy belting out songs old and new. It was also good to catch up with Jo Laing, lighting up the event as she usually does.

The thing about Vegas is you never really feel tired there (due in no small part to the lack of clocks, windows and the amount of oxygen they pump into the casinos) so the drinking went long into the night.

I did manage to sneak out and do a few things (visit the Pawn Stars, Mob Museum and go to see tributes to Elvis and Sinatra) but my personal highlight away from the convention was going out with the New Orleans Stephens, Patterson and Holzenthal, for a steak in Circus Circus. The two of these guys sum up Celtic, thousands of miles from Celtic Park but feeling it every bit as much as someone who resides in the Gallowgate.

Of course you see plenty folk you know at the convention whilst others you see on social media every day but never actually bump into. That's how big these things are.

The main event is the Dinner Dance on the Friday. I was in helping set up things about 4pm on the day and the sheer scale of the place, decorated in Celtic flags, took my breath away. 6000 miles from where the team play, a celebration of Celtic was about to engulf Las Vegas like The Rat Pack used to.

All of this is due to the committee of The Fed and unsung heroes like Peter Milligan who, like Tam and Mike, aren't there for a holiday.

A fantastic night was had by all and a lot of people were still partying when the Ireland v Scotland match started at 9am the next day (a match which raised over $3000 for The Kano Foundation as well which Joe Mackin went on stage and humbly received) and finally gave Stephen Rodgers a real chance to wear his constant kilt.

Saturday is the day when a few folk start to drift away and things start to wind down just a tad. No shock really as either the liver says "enough" or the bank balance says "no more".

Unfortunately one of those guys was Rik Roberts from Detroit, who is always a welcome face at any Celtic event.

They came from everywhere for this convention, Tokyo, Sydney, Denver and Castlemilk but everyone the same, smiling faces and big Celtic hearts.

I left on the Sunday, head pounding from a major sesh in The Flamingo and, when I walked into the taxi, the porter opening the door for me said "Have a safe trip and Hail Hail!"

This guy probably didn't know who Celtic were this time last week.

Everyone in The Westgate does now.

Prologue 2.0-Is this the end? Or just the beginning...

This book changed my life. In many ways. I lost a dear friend because of it, I became a hate figure because of it, I had my life threatened on numerous occasions because of it, I found out what a few people are really about because of it and I became persona non grata among some Celtic supporters who don't like folk from my class background writing books about Celtic. On the other hand, I paid bills because of it, I heated my house because of it, I was able to provide for my kids because of it, I got incredible support from Celtic supporters because of it and I was able to travel the world showing I film I made that was based on the book.

What I've tried to do in this book is show you that whilst our club was being plotted against and schemed about, cheated and obstructed at every opportunity by men who lived with the trappings of wealth, access and power and all within a five mile radius, there were Bhoys and Ghirls all over the place who had nothing but fought them every step of the way and won. I was one of them and I just happened to stay a Bobo Balde clearance away from the Axis of Evil that exists in Edinburgh but I lived in a different world entirely, I think I've shown you that. That was deliberate on their part of course. Their whole system, their whole make up was about keeping people like us as far away from them as possible. The mistake they made was they walked into our arena, football grounds. People like us don't take too kindly to someone coming into our house and pushing us around. I'm just a very minor character in that respect. I do what I can in books, blogs, podcasts and any platform that I can.

Men like Fergus McCann, Tommy Burns, Martin O'Neill and Neil Lennon stood up to them and refused to buckle. Millions of Celtic supporters, derided and called paranoid for decades refused to lie down and came back at them like a caged animal and ended up ripping the lot of them to pieces.

That's no mean feat.

Many of you, if not all, who read this will know me. I am many things, not all good, but the one thing I am proud to say is not only am I a Celtic supporter but I am a Celtic supporter who was there at the beginning of the asterisk years and was there at the end of the asterisk years too.

It wasn't easy and this club (and writing books for that matter) have cost me a lot, things you can never get back, no matter how hard you try and it's normally too late before you realise that.

So the question is, was it worth it?

Was it worth keeping going to all the games, sacrificing relationships, friends, families, education and holidays to Spain or wherever the fuck it is people go these days.

As I sit here writing this now, alone in my flat, after a terrible day that I just told people on Facebook about and a blood pressure check up to come tomorrow, it would be easy to say no, it wasn't worth it.

But I'd be lying wouldn't I? Because if I said that, then it wouldn't be me, would it?

I've given you a light-hearted look at my life in the midst of a conspiracy to destroy our football club. Those stories are a bit of fun for me, hopefully for you too. I've made it look like all the bad things that have happened to me in life are because someone deliberately fucked me over or I was born with a shit covered spoon in my mouth. That happened a lot but a lot of things I fucked myself, I put my hands up to that (a stupid thing to do when typing, let me tell you)

I also lived a lot of my life thinking there was a dedicated group of people who would do anything to destroy Celtic and I hope that with this book, the inner workings contained within and the tales from our referee friend, I have proved that beyond a reasonable doubt.

Be happy my friends, we won the war, we took everything they could throw at us and still emerged victorious.

(Brief interlude to dance a little jig)

So, was it worth it?

Don't be daft, if you've got this far in the book then you're like me, you didn't have a choice.

The other thing is, since this book came out in October 2013, there have been many changes and things happened. David Murray no longer resides in Murrayfield. His vanity office in Charlotte Square belongs to someone else and last I heard he was flogging wine in the Far East and building houses in Newhouse. His well-heeled friends are few and far between now. Many of them, like Angus Grossart for example, see him as toxic. His Murray Group business was broken up and hived off to "family members" whilst the pension fund he ran was last known to have debts of £22m.

Cheating is cheating is cheating.

Lance Armstrong, Barry Bonds, Ben Johnson, Rangers. They all cheated to get an unfair sporting advantage.

On every angle you want to look at, Rangers cheated.

In fact, it was the biggest organised cheating scandal in the history of Scottish football and David Murray was responsible for it all.

The Tax Tribunal describes him: "While Mr Black(sic) had been involved in 'signing and selling' 350-400 players in 20 years of involvement at Rangers, he had not, and could not, because of all his commitments, devote any real time to detailed contractual negotiations. At the start of each football season he would meet with his manager to decide on which players might be possible recruits."

He wasn't duped. Nor was his neighbour Lord Nimmo-Smith.

Why were credit lines needed? Why were cosy overdrafts sought? Why was tax avoided?

One reason.

Sporting advantage.

The End-One afternoon in Lisbon

A little bit of fun. One of the things that kept me going throughout *The Asterisk Years*, as the knockers and begrudgers circled like vultures eyeing a decaying body in the desert, I was working away at something that started off akin to going to Mars yet ended up happening.

The Asterisk Years screened at the Estadio Nacional in Lisbon.

It is hard to put into words what this meant to me but I'll try. It all started when a well-known Celtic legend put the idea to me back in March. I laughed and thought it fanciful but then two wonderful guys from Portugal, Carlos and Jose, were on the case and this looked like it could actually happen. There were a few things I had to do at this end, supplying signed shirts, signed balls and various other Celtic goodies for the guys so favours were called in more than Don Corleone.

The date was set, Sunday June 21st. Arriving at the stadium, I tried to soak it all in. It was a lovely, calm day and I was met by Carlos and Jose in the building next to the park after a short cab ride in from Saldanha. They spoke good English, which was a help obviously, but had assembled a team of entirely non English speakers.

One guy did manage a "2-1" with his fingers (at least I hope that's what it was) and we moved around the running track, past the stairs where the Lions famously belted out The Celtic Song, and into a sort of conference room.

I was told we had one hour and that suited me fine.

As the film started, the guys smiled but I'm not going to lie, as it went on I don't think any of them had any idea what they were watching. Also, I didn't care.

All my mind was on was getting at least one photo at the side of the park.

The film finished and a series of awkward handshakes took place akin to meeting your future in laws for the first time. After that though, the cherry on the icing, I had the run of the stadium.

The iPod was out and photos galore were taken, loads of those ones where you're standing there and wondering why the feck the person hasn't pushed the button yet but we got there in the end.

Bliss is something I've experienced a couple of times in life and I experienced it on that day, for most of the day. You see the hour was just for the room, I could stay in the stadium as long as I wanted and so I did. I walked round it three times, covered every blade of grass, sat in a lot of seats and stood where King Billy McNeill rose the big cup aloft and shot Celtic out in front of a race against Rangers that would end with us winning and them dying.

And so *The Asterisk Years* project ended where the story began, in the heat of Lisbon.